A NEW ELEMENTARY
TEACHINGS OF ISLAM

Maulana Mohammed Abdul-Aleem Siddiqui

A NEW ELEMENTARY TEACHINGS OF ISLAM

Maulana Mohammed Abdul-Aleem Siddiqui

Published in the UK by Beacon Books and Media Ltd,
60 Farringdon Road, London EC1R 3GA
www.beaconbooks.net

Copyright © Beacon Books and Media Ltd, 2014

Printed in the UK

ISBN 978-0-9926335-3-0

A CIP catalogue record for this book is available from the British Library.

TABLE OF CONTENTS

Publisher's Note ix
Preface to the Third Edition x
About the Author xiii
Introduction 1
Part I 3
Iman -Belief 4

   Oneness of Allah 5

   Angels 6

   The Books of Allah 8

   The Prophets of Allah 10

   Day of Resurrection and the Day of Judgment 12

   The Power of Doing Good or Evil 13

PART II 15
Islam 16

   The Declaration of Faith 17

   Kalima-e-Tayyibah كَلِمَه طَيِّبَه 17

   Kalimatush-Shahaadat كَلِمَةُ الشَّهَا دَةِ 17

   Kalimatut-Tamjeed كَلِمَةُ التَّمْجِيْد 18

   Kalimatut-Tahmeed كَلِمَةُ التَّحْمِيْد 18

   Kalimatus-tighfaar كَلِمَةُ اسْتِغْفَار 19

   Kalimatu-Raddi-kufr كَلِمَةُ رَدِّ كُفْر 19

   Who is Muhammad? 21

   Prayer الصلوة 23

   Wudu الوضوْ 25

The Obligatory Acts in the Performance of Wudu   28
Ghusl غسل   29
Tayammum تيمم   30
Miscellaneous Notes   32
Azan اذان   34
Fajr Azan   35
Iqama اقامة   36
The Obligatory and Essential Factors of Prayer   37

Performing the Prayer   39

A Complete Description of the Prayer   39
Sajdatus-Sahw   48
Classification of Prayer   49
Fard Prayers   51
Waajib-Ul-Witr   53
Salaatul-Janaazah   54
Salaat-Ul-Musaafir   57
Salaatul-Jumu'a   58
Salaatut-Taraaweeh   59
Waajibul 'Id   60
Nafl Prayers   62
Forbidden Times for Prayer   63
Miscellaneous   65
Zakat   66
Sadaqatul-Fitr   68
Fasting   69
Al Hajj   72
Tawaf   77
Sa'ee   81
The Performance of Hajj   83
Umra   85

vi

PART III   *89*
Poetry   *89*

    God is only One   *90*
    God is Just   *91*
    A Second Guide   *92*
    Books of God   *94*
    Judgement Day   *95*
    The Five Pillars   *96*
    The Prophet of Islam   *97*

PUBLISHER'S NOTE

It has been almost 65 years since the first edition of this book was published by Haji Mohammed Ibrahim in 1950 in the West Indian Island of Trinidad under the title of *A Short Catechism of Islam for Elementary Level Students*. The title was later changed to *A Short Catechism of Islam for the First Teachings of Islam* and by the 3rd edition in 1954 and thereafter it was known as *Elementary Teachings of Islam*. Since then it has undergone numerous edition by a wide range of publishers from the far West in the Caribbean Islands to the Far East in Singapore which is host to the Grand Mosque named after our esteemed author Maulana Mohammed Abdul-Aleem Siddiqui (1892-1956).

The book was originally written in a question and answer format which was the standard form of instruction in the Indian sub-continent, particularly to very young children. However we felt that this format was not suitable for a modern audience and so we removed the questions and left a simple narrative that is much easier to follow. This then accounts for the change in the title of the book to *A New* Elementary Teachings of Islam.

We are grateful to the Association of Islamic Charitable Projects in North America who generously allowed the use of the illustrations used to show the positions in Wudu and Prayer.

We hope our efforts in reviving this classic text is of some use and benefit to our readers who may be new to Islam or those wanting to get a good understanding of the fundamentals of Islam for the first time.

Publisher

PREFACE TO THE THIRD EDITION

It is a living miracle of the Truth of Islam that, though it has neither the backing of huge missionary corporations, nor does it have any authentic literature in foreign languages, yet people after people, attracted to it by its inherent, magnetic force, keep on embracing this religion of love and universal brotherhood. For, whenever either by dint of personal research and study or by a chance contact with, and the consequent guidance of a real Muslim theologian, they learn the true facts about Islam, the invariable conclusion they arrive at is that Islam is a very simple religion and all its teachings are perfectly rational and in complete consonance with the laws of nature.

Islam is not a new religion, but a divinely-executed combination of all the old inspired ones and provides via the media, the golden means. On the one hand, its comprehensively high code of ethics, which is unique for many reasons, equips its follower for his journey towards the ultimate goal of a sincere seeker after Truth, Allah; and, on the other, directs its followers to foster and maintain fraternal relations with all the human beings and achieve the utmost progress in all the spheres of art and science and the material walks of life.

This is the only religion, the Sacred Book of which, the Holy Qur'an, is preserved intact in its pristine purity and an authentic record of the minutest details of the eventful life of its promulgator, Prophet Muhammad (May peace and blessings of

Allah be on him), is extant to this day after a lapse of more than thirteen centuries.

The necessity of the presentation of 'The Elementary Teachings of Islam', explaining its cardinal articles of faith and the fundamental principles in the simplest possible English language is, therefore, obvious; for such a publication would not only serve to acquaint the English speaking new Muslims with the essentials of Faith and the directions for engaging in devotion to Allah, but also supply the long felt need of a handy book for imparting the rudiments of Islam to the Muslim children of those countries where the English language rules supreme and children are sent away to school using English as medium of instruction, without having any knowledge, whatsoever, of their religion.

Realising the urgency of publishing such a volume, I, during my itinerary of Ceylon, Singapore, Penang, Java, etc., drafted out a skeleton according to the Shafi'i School inspite of numerous preoccupations. My learned friend, Mr. M.I.M. Haniffa, B.A. (London), Advocate of Colombo, very kindly undertook to revise and touch it up, and it was due to his invaluable assistance that 'A Short Catechism of the First Teachings of Islam' was published a few years ago, and has proved very beneficial.

About the same time an incomplete and imperfect draft, according to the Hanafi School, was released for publication in "The Real Islam" of Singapore on account of pressing demands. The present volume is a thoroughly revised and enlarged edition of that draft. While sending it to the press, I feel, I must acknowledge the co-operation, in this humble work, of Mr. K.S. Anwari, my Secretary, during the South and East African tour, and of my son-in-law Hafiz Muhammad Fazlur Rahman Ansari, B.A. (Alig.).

While expressing the hope that this little volume will serve the purpose in view and will meet the approval of all those concerned, 1 desire to record my sincere thanks to Al-Haj Muhammad Ibrahim of Trinidad for liberally undertaking the cost of printing and thus rendering a signal service to Islam and to the public.

If it pleases Allah, a second volume, in which common sense arguments in support of the cardinal articles of faith and a much more detailed treatment of the principles of Islam and the laws governing society will be incorporated, will soon follow this modest attempt.

May it please Allah to accept this humble service, Ameen!

ABOUT THE AUTHOR

Maulana Mohammed Abdul-Aleem Siddiqui (Rahma-tullah Ta'ala Alaih), a direct descendent of the first Caliph Syedna Siddique Akbar (Radiallaho Anhu) was born in Meerut, India in 1892. His father Maulana Abdul Hakeem was a great scholar of his time. His son, the late Maulana Shah Ahmad Noorani continued the family tradition of scholarly excellence and travelling around the world to propagate the message of Islam. Maulana was also an excellent orator and singer of naats (religious poetry) and was well versed in Arabic, French, English, Persian, Swahili, African, German and Urdu.

After completing his education, Maulana decided to spread the light of Islam around the world. The countries he visited include Burma, Ceylon, china, Japan, U.K. , USA, Canada, Egypt, Iran, Iraq, Libya, Algeria, Sudan, Yemen, Syria, Tunis, Lebanon, Malaysia, Indonesia, Singapore, Thailand, Saudi Arab, Jordan, South Africa, South America, East Africa, Tanzania, East Indies, West Indies, Kenya, Philistine, Philippine, Fiji, Portugal, Tanzania, Zanzibar, Vietnam, Bangladesh, Sri Lanka, Belgium,

Germany, France, Italy, Mauritius, Madagascar, Reunion, Guiana, Uganda, Congo, Trinidad etc.

In his missionary tours His Eminence did not confine himself to the preaching of Islam but along with the cooperation of local Muslims, laid foundation of mosques, madrassahs, schools and colleges, orphanages, hospitals, hostels for converts societies, libraries, scout groups, volunteer corpse etc. More than 50,000 non-Muslims embraced Islam at the pious hands of His Eminence.

In 1935 His Eminence had a meeting with the famous Irish playright, George Bernard Shaw who was one of the most famous western intellectuals of his age. He showed remarkable respect for Prophet Muhammad (s) and there was manifest sincerity in the courteous way in which he greeted, met and parted from the eminent scholar of Islam.

His Eminence died at the age of 63 in the holy city of Madinatul Munawarrah and was buried under the footsteps of Bibi Ayesha Siddiqua (Radiallahu Anha) in Jannatul Baqee Al Shareef. May Almighty Allah shower the most precious blessings upon his grave day and night and give him the best place in Jannatul Firdous. Aameen summa amen.

INTRODUCTION

Allah created me you and all the worlds. Allah created us all but He is not created by anyone. Our duty to Allah is to have complete faith (Iman) in Him and to submit ourselves entirely to His commands. We can have knowledge about Him and His commands through His apostles and prophets.

An apostle or a prophet is a very true and pious man. He is chosen by Allah as His messenger. Allah inspires him with His commands, and he conveys them to humanity. In this way, we may know the right path to lead a good life in this world and, thus pleasing Allah, may attain peace after death.

Prophets were sent by Allah to all nations whenever and wherever there was a need for them. When all the nations were in need of one, Allah sent Prophet Muhammad for the whole world.

Prophet Muhammad has taught us to render complete submission to the commands of Allah, which is called Islam. What are the cardinal articles of faith in Islam?

The cardinal articles of faith in Islam are seven in number:

1. To believe in the Oneness of Allah.
2. To believe in all His angels.
3. To believe in all His books.
4. To believe in all His prophets.
5. To believe in the Day of Resurrection.
6. To believe in the Day of Judgment. (Sometimes combined with previous article.)

7. To believe that the power of doing all actions (whether good or bad) proceeds from Allah, but that we are responsible for our actions.

The fundamental principles of Islam are five in number:

1. The declaration of Laa ilahaa illallaah Muhammadur-Rasoolullah, meaning: There is no god but Allah, and Muhammad is His prophet.
2. The observance of the obligatory prayers five times a day.
3. Distribution of Zakat (Islamic alms-fee) among the deserving amounting to one fortieth in one's possession for a complete year.
4. The observation of fasts during the day time in the month of Ramadan.
5. The performance of Hajj (pilgrimage) to Makkah, at least once in a lifetime, if circumstances permit.

In the following section of the book we will consider in more detail the seven cardinal articles of faith and in part two we will explain in detail the five fundamental principles of Islam.

PART I

The Cardinal Articles of Faith Iman

IMAN -BELIEF

اَمَنْتُ بِا للهِ وَمَلَٰٓئِكَتِهِ وَ كُتُبِهِ وَ رُسُلِهِ وَالْيَوْ مِ ا لْاٰ خِرِ وَالْقَدْرِ خَيْرِ هِ
وَ شَرِّهِ مِنَ اللهِ تَعَالٰى وَالْبَعْثِ بَعْدَ الْمَوْ تِ ۝

Aamantu Billaahi wa Malaaikatihee wa Kutubihee wa Rusulihee wal
Yuamil Akhiree walquadri Khairihee wa Sharriee Minallaahi T'aalaa
walb'athi Ba'dal maut.

I affirm my belief in Allah and His angels and His books and His
messengers and on the Day of Judgment and all good things that
come from Allah and those that are destined to me and all evil
things that come from Allah being destined to me and in the
Resurrection, that is coming to life again after death.

CHAPTER 1
ONENESS OF ALLAH

Belief in the Oneness of Allah, means that Allah is One and there is none like Him; He has no partner; He neither begets nor is He begotten; He is indivisible in person; He is Eternal; He is Infinite; He has neither beginning nor end; He is Almighty, the All-Knowing, the All-just, the Cherisher of all worlds, the Patron, the Guide, the Helper, the Merciful, the Compassionate, etc.

Allah is everywhere. Allah knows all the actions I do on earth, both good and bad. He even knows your secret thoughts. Allah has created us and all the worlds. He loves and cherishes us one and all. He will reward us in Heaven for all our good actions and punish us in Hell for all our evil deeds.

We can win the love of Allah by complete submission to His Will and obedience to His Commands. We can know the Will and Commands of Allah from the Holy Qur'an and from the Traditions of our Prophet Muhammad (May peace and blessings of Allah be upon him).

Iman means 'to believe in', i.e. to have a firm and sincere belief in the cardinal articles of faith. Islam means 'complete submission', i.e. submitting to the orders of Allah and acting in accordance with His Commands. One who professes Iman is called a Mu'min (The Faithful), and one who observes all the principles of Islam is called a Muslim.

CHAPTER 2

ANGELS

Angels are spiritual creatures of Allah, ever obedient to His Will and Commands. They are neither males nor females; they have neither parents, nor wives, nor husbands, nor sons, nor daughters. They have no material bodies, but can assume any form they like.

Angels do not eat and drink like human beings, nor do they enjoy sleep. The most important Angels of Allah are four in number:

1. Jibreel جِبْرِيْل
2. Mika'il مِيْکَائِيْل
3. Israfeel اِسْرَافِيْل
4. Izra'eel عِزْرَائِيْل

There are many other angels, some of whom mentioned in the Qur'an are known to us, but we have no knowledge about the number, names and duties of others, which are known only to Allah.

Angel Jibreel was employed by Allah to convey the Messages to His Chosen Ones on earth, the apostles and the prophets, who appeared in all ages and all climes. It was the Angel Jibreel who communicated the revelations of Allah to our Prophet Muhammad (May peace and blessings of Allah be upon him).

The main qualities of angels are purity, righteousness, truthfulness and obedience to the Will and Commands of Allah. Angels only act in obedience to the Commands of Allah; hence they cannot do anything on earth without His order. We do not worship the angels at all. We adore and pray to Allah alone. Angels are the servants of Allah and they too worship Him. The Holy Qur'an explicitly says that we should neither worship anyone but Allah nor should we associate any partner with Him.

CHAPTER 3

THE BOOKS OF ALLAH

Allah revealed Commandments and Codes of religion to various Prophets at different stages of history for the guidance of mankind. The Codes of Religion or the Books of Allah are four in number:

1. Taurat (Old Testament) تورات

2. Zaboor (Psalms) زبور

3. Injeel (New Testament) انجيل

4. The Holy Qur'an قرآن مجيد

The Taurat was revealed to Prophet Moosa (Moses), Zaboor to Prophet Dawood (David), Injeel to Prophet Isa (Jesus), and the Holy Qur'an to Prophet Muhammad (may peace and blessings of Allah be upon them all). The Taurat, Zaboor and Injeel do not exist in their original forms. The present-day editions are only interpretations by their respective followers of later ages. As Muslims we follow the last Code of Religion, the Holy Qur'an.

The Holy Qur'an is the Gospel of the religion of Islam. The previous Commandments and the Codes of Religion are also incorporated in it. Its verses were inspired and revealed by Allah to Prophet Muhammad through Angel Jibreel, and they are still preserved intact in their original form in the Arabic language. The verses of the Holy Qur'an were revealed to Prophet Muhammad either singly or in batches during the last twenty-three years of his life, and were written down at his dictation and arranged under his direction during his lifetime.

The Holy Qur'an teaches us to worship Almighty Allah, Him and Him alone, to obey His orders contained therein, to follow the teachings and examples set by Prophet Muhammad, to do good to others, especially to our parents and relations, and to be honest and truthful in all my actions and dealings, in short, it gives us a complete code for the rightful guidance of our lives.

CHAPTER 4

THE PROPHETS OF ALLAH

At different stages of the history of mankind, Allah sent prophets as His messengers for the guidance of mankind. We believe in all of them in general, and in those whose names are mentioned in the Holy Qur'an in particular. We cannot personify anyone as a prophet if his name is not so mentioned in the Divine Book, nor can we deny the prophethood of anyone whose name is so mentioned in the Divine Book.

We do not know the names of all the prophets who delivered the message of Allah to mankind, but the names of the great prophets are mentioned in the Holy Qur'an. Among the prophets whose names are mentioned in the Holy Qur'an are: Adam, Idrees (Enoch), Noah, Hood, Saleh, Ibrahim (Abraham), Isma'il (Ishmael), Ishaq (Isaac), Ya'qoob (Jacob), Yusuf (Joseph), Ayyoob(Job), Shu'aib, Moosa (Moses), Haroon (Aaron), Loot (Lot), Yoonus (Jonah), AI-Yas'a, Zulkifl, Dawood (David), Sulaiman (Solomon), Ilyas (Elias), Zakaria (Zechariah), Yahya, Isa (Jesus) and Muhammad.

A prophet is a servant and messenger of Allah who receives the divine revelations. He is a model for human beings and teaches and practices the Commands of Allah. The most important from among these prophets are: Adam, Noah, Ibrahim, Moosa, 'Isa and the last and the greatest of all Prophets, Muhammad (may peace and blessings of Allah be upon them all.

We do not worship any of the prophets, but only love and revere them and consider them as models of conduct for myself as well as humanity at large. The prophets themselves worshipped Allah and taught us to do the same. None of the prophets can be called God, for they were all created by Allah Who is Self-Existing and has no partner. None of the prophets claimed divinity, for, besides being messengers and servants of Allah, they themselves were human beings.

As all the nations of the world had either lost or forgotten the Messages delivered by the Prophets sent to them, Prophet Muhammad proclaimed the Message of Allah to all lands and to all nations. His Prophethood is, therefore, not confined to any one land or one nation, but is universal, i.e. for the whole world and for all the nations.

There is no need of a prophet after Prophet Muhammad, for the Message, i.e. the Holy Qur'an (that he has brought for the whole world) is the final and the completes code of religion, and is and will be preserved for all time absolutely intact in its original form; besides the authentic record of the Prophet's eventual life covering all human activities is also extant, and will always remain as a model for mankind. Hence no prophet either with code and commandments, or without, is required after him, and therefore the Holy Qur'an says that Prophet Muhammad is the last and the Seal of all prophets.

CHAPTER 5

DAY OF RESURRECTION AND THE DAY OF JUDGMENT

The Day of Resurrection and Judgment is the day on which Allah will resurrect the dead, i.e. make the dead live again. He will then judge each person according to his good or bad actions on earth. He will reward those who have led a righteous life and pleased Him, by sending them to Heaven, and punish those who have disobeyed His Commands and incurred His displeasure by committing sins and bad actions, by consigning them to Hell.

Heaven is an abode of peace and happiness where every wish is fulfilled. Hell is a place of torture, pain and agony. A person who dies with complete faith in the Oneness of Allah and in the Prophets of Allah will remain in Heaven for ever, while a person who dies without having any belief in the Oneness of Allah and in the Prophets of Allah or having belief in others as partners of Allah will remain in Hell for ever.

Those who have firm belief in the Oneness of Allah and in the Prophets of Allah but die without atoning for and repenting sins they have committed in this world will be sent to Hell for a time, from where, after receiving due punishment, they will be liberated by the mercy of Allah and sent to Heaven, where they will live for ever.

CHAPTER 6

THE POWER OF DOING GOOD OR EVIL

Allah has given us the power of action (good or bad), but He has also given us reason and a code of life to choose between good and evil, and therefore, we are responsible for our actions. For example, Allah has given us the power of speaking. It is for us to use the tongue for speaking the truth or abuse its power by speaking lies.

Allah helps us to do good acts by sending messengers to guide us all along the right path and codes of religion. Any action against the commands of Allah is a sin and Allah alone can forgive sins. In order that our sins be forgiven, we must pray to Allah with all our heart and, atoning for all our evil deeds, resolve never to commit any such or other misdeeds again.

The articles of food and drink that have been decreed unlawful for a Muslim are:
1. All kinds of intoxicating wines, liquors and spirits.
2. Flesh of swine and all wild animals that employ claws or teeth for killing their victims, e.g. tigers, leopards, elephants, wolves, etc., and all birds of prey as hawks, eagles, vultures, crows, etc.
3. Rodents, reptiles, worms, etc.

4. Flesh of dead animals that are otherwise sanctioned as legitimate.

5. Flesh of animals and birds (sanctioned) that are not slaughtered or slayed in the prescribed manner.

6. Flesh of animals that are offered as sacrifice to idols.

The method of slaughtering animal or a bird whose flesh is sanctioned to be lawful for food is quite simple. One should say بِسْمِ اللهِ اَ للهُ اَ كْبَر 'Bismillahi Allahu-Akbar' at the time of slaughtering and pass the knife over its throat in such a manner that the main arteries are out as under, but the spinal chord is left alone for a while till all the blood oozes out.

Some of the acts that are major sins and are liable for severe punishment are:

1. To believe in anyone as partner of Allah.

2. To disbelieve in Allah or His Prophets or His Books, or to deny any of the fundamental principles of Islam.

3. To lie.

4. To commit adultery or sodomy

5. To rob or steal

6. To cheat or deceive anyone.

7. To bear false witness.

8. To bring false charge against anyone.

9. To backbite.

10. To abuse anybody or injure anyone's feelings.

With this we have now completed our explanation of the cardinal articles of faith in Islam. We will now consider the five fundamental principles of Islam.

PART II

The Fundamental Principles of Islam

ISLAM

بُنِىَ الْإِسْلَامُ عَلَى خَمْسٍ شَهَادَةِ أَنْ لَّا اِلٰهَ اِلَّا اللّٰهُ وَاَنَّ مُحَمَّدً رَّسُوْلُ اللّٰهِ وَاِقَامِ الصَّلٰوةِ وَاِيْتَآ ِالزَّكٰوةِ وَصَوْمِ رَمْضَانَ وَ حِجِّ الْبَيْتِ مَنِ اسْتَطَاعَ اِلَيْهِ سَبِيْلٌ ۞

Buniyal lslaamu'alaa Khamsin Shahaadati Al-laa-ilaaha Illallaahu wa Anna Muhammadar Rasoolullaahi wa lqaamissalaati wa leetaaizzakaati wa Saumi Ramadaana wa Hijjil Baiyti Manistataa'a Ilaiyhi Sabilaa.

'The faith of Islam is based on five fundamental principles; first in the belief that there is no God but Allah and Muhammad Sallallaahu Alaiyhi wasallam is the Messenger of Allah, second to establish obligatory prayers (Salat), third to pay the Zakat (Poor-due), fourth to observe fast during the Holy Month of Ramadhan and fifth to perform Hajj that is Pilgrimage to the Holy Ka'aba in Makkah if one is financially capable of undertaking the journey to Makkah.'

CHAPTER I
THE DECLARATION OF FAITH

Kalima-e-Tayyibah كَلِمَه طَيِّبَه

The first principle of Islam is to declare:

لَآاِلَهَ اِلَّااللّٰهُ مُحَمَّدٌرَّسُوْلُ اللّٰهِ

Laa ilaaha illallaahu Muhammadur-rasoolullaah.

'There is no Deity but Allah, and Muhammad is the Apostle of Allah.'

There are five other forms of the declaration of faith:

Kalimatush-Shahaadat كَلِمَةُ الشَّهَا دَةِ

Declaration or Submission of Evidence

اَشْهَدُ اَنْ لَآ اِ لَهَ اِلَّا اللّٰهُ وَحْدَهُ لَآ شَرِيْکَ لَهُ وَ اَ شْهَدُ اَنَّ مُحَمَّدًاعَبْدُهُ
وَ رَسُوْلُهُ

Ashhadu al Laa ilaaha illallaahu wahdahu Laa shareeka lahu wa ashhadu anna Muhammadan abduhoo wa rasooluh.

'I bear witness that there is no Deity but Allah, Who is without partner, and l bear witness that Muhammad is His servant and apostle.'

Kalimatut-Tamjeed كَلِمَةُ التَّمْجِيْد

Declaration of the Glory of Allah

سُبْحَانَ اللهِ وَالْحَمْدُ لِلهِ وَلَا اِلٰهَ اِلَّا اللهُ وَاللهُ اَكْبَرُ وَلَا حَوْلَ وَلَا قُوَّةَ
الْعَظِيْمِ اِلَّا بِا للهِ الْعَلِّي

Subhaanallaahi Walhamdu lillaahi wa laa ilaaha illallaahu wallaahu
Akbar, wa laa haula wa laa quwwata illaa billaahil 'Aliyyil' Azeem.

'Glory be to Allah and praise, there is no Deity but Allah, Allah is
Most Great, there is no power, no might but from Allah, the Most
High, the Great.'

Kalimatut-Tahmeed كَلِمَةُ التَّحْمِيْد

Declaration of the Oneness of Allah

لَاۤاِلٰهَ اِلَّا اللهُ وَحْدَهُ لَا شَرِيْكَ لَهُ ۔ لَهُ الْمُلْكُ وَلَهُ الْحَمْدُ يُحْى وَيُمِيْتُ
وَهُوَ حَيٌّ لَا يَمُوْ تُ اَبَدًا اَبَدًا ۞ ذُوالْجَلَالِ وَالْاِكْرَامِ بِيَدِهِ الْخَيْرُ ۔ وَهُوَ عَلٰى
كُلِّ شَئٍ قَدِيْرٌ

Laailaaha illallaahu wahdahu Laa Shareeka lahoo Lahul mulku wa lahul
Hamdu Yuhyee wa Yumeetu wa huwa Hayyullaa Yamootu Abadan Abadaa
Zuljalaali wal ikraam Biyadihil Khairu wa huwa alaa kulli Shai-in Qadeer.

'There is none to be worshipped save Allah; He is Alone, none is
to be associated to Him. His is the Kingdom of the whole
Universe and for Him is the entire Praise. Only He gives life and
causes death, and He is Living and death will never come to Him.
He is Majestic and All-Dignified. In His Hand is all good and He
has power over all things.'

Kalimatus-tighfaar كَلِمَةُ اسْتِغْفَار

اَسْتَغْفِرُاللّٰه رَبِّى مِنْ كُلِّ ذَنْبِ اَذْنَبْتُهُ عَمَدًا اَوْ خَطَأً سِرًّا اَوْعَلَا نِيَّةً
وَاَتُوبُ اِلَيْهِ مِنَ الذَّنْبِ الَّذِىْ لَآ اَعْلَمُ اِنَّكَ اَنْتَ عَلَّا ، الْغُيُوْبِ وَ سَتَّا رُ ا
لْعُيُوْ بِ وَ غَفَّا رُ الذُّنُوْ بِ وَلَا حَوْلَ وَلَا قُوَّةَ اِلَّا بِاللّٰهِ الْعَلِّى الْعَظِيْمِ

Astaghfirullaaha Rabbee Min Kulli Zambin Aznabtuhoo Amadan au
Khataa'an Sir-ran Au alaaniyatanw wa Atoobu ilaiyhi minazzambillazee
A'lamu wa minazzambillazee laa A'lamu innaka Anta Allaamulghuyoobi
wa Sattaarul Uyoobi wa ghaffaaruzzunoobi walaa Haula walaa Quwwata
illaa billaahil Aliyyil Azeem.

'l ask forgiveness of Allah, Who is my Cherisher, for all the sins l
committed knowingly or unknowingly, secretly or publicly and l
repent towards Him of the sins which I am aware of and for the
sins which l am not aware of. Undoubtedly You are the Best
Knower of all unseen things and the conceiler of the wrongdoings
and the Best Forgiver of the sins; and there is no power, no might
(of doing all actions whether good or evil) but with the help of
Allah, the Most Exalted, the Great.'

Kalimatu-Raddi-kufr كَلِمَةُ رَدِّ كُفْر

Declaration of the Refutation of Disbelief

اَ لّٰهُمَّ اِنِّى اَ عُوْذُبِكَ مِنْ اَنْ اُشْرِكَ بِكَ شَيْأً وَّاَ نَا اَ عْلَمُ
بِهِ اَسْتَغْفِرُكَ لِمَآ لَآ اَعْلَمُ بِهِ تُبْتُ عَنْهُ وَ تَبَرَّاتُ مِنَ الْكُفْرِ وَ الشِّرْكِ
وَالْكِذْبِ وَالْغِيْبَةِ وَالْبِدْعَةِ وَالنَّمِيْمَةِ وَالْفَوَاحِشِ وَالْبُهْتَانِ وَالْمَعَاصِىْ كُلِّهَا
وَاَسْلَمْتُ وَاَقُوْلُ لَا اِلٰهَ اِلَّا اللّٰهُ مُحَمَّدٌ رَّسُوْلُ اللّٰهِ

Allaahumma innee a'oozu bika min an ushrika bika shai'anw, wa anaa
a'lamu wa astaghfiruka limaa laa A'lamu bihee tubtu anhu wa
tabarraa'tu minalkufri washshirki wal kizbi wal gheebati wal bid'ati wan
nameemati wal fawaahishi wal buh taani wal ma'aasi kulli haa wa aslam
tu wa aqoolu laa ilaaha illaiiaahu Muhammad-ur-rasool-ullaah.

19

'O Allah! verily do I seek refuge in Thee from associating any partner with Thee knowingly; and I beseech the forgiveness for the sins which I am not aware of and I repented of it. And I free myself of infidelity and polytheism and falsehood and backbiting and sinful innovation and telling lies and all other sins, and I have entered the fold of Islam, and thereby declare: There is no Deity but Allah, and Muhammad is the Apostle of Allah.'

Who is Muhammad?

Muhammad is the Rasool, i.e. the Messenger and Prophet of Allah who received the Message from Allah through divine revelation and conveyed the same to humanity. He was born in Makkah in Arabia and is descended from Prophet Abraham. He was the son of Abdullah, who was the son of 'Abdul Muttalib, who was son of Hashim, who was the son of 'Abd Manaf.

Abdullah, the Prophet's father died before his birth, and he lost his mother, Amina, during his infancy. He was, then, for a short time under the care of his grandfather, 'Abdul Muttalib, who also died a few years later. His uncle, Abu Talib, then, became his guardian. He did not receive any instruction through human agency. His education was solely due to Divine Sources.

The Message of Allah was first revealed to our Prophet through angel Jibreel (Gabriel), at the age of fourty, in the cave at the foot of Mt. Hira in Makkah. The people of Makkah had a very great regard for him. They honoured and respected him for his integrity and honesty, and were so impressed by them and the nobility and gentleness of his character that they conferred upon him the title of the Trustworthy, before he proclaimed his Prophethood.

The people of Makkah in general did not accept Muhammad as a prophet, when he first delivered to them the Message of Allah against idols and idolatry. Only a few embraced Islam. Others persecuted him and his followers so much that he, along with his followers, was compelled to seek refuge in Medina.

The migration of our Prophet from Makkah to Medina is called Al Hijra. The Muslim calendar commences from the day of this migration. Most of the people of Medina received our Prophet with kindness, believed in his teaching and mission and embraced Islam.

Our Prophet died at the age of sixty-three and was buried in Medina, where his tomb now stands. We should visit the tomb of our Prophet at Medina, preferably after the performance of Hajj (Pilgrimage) to Makkah, for our Prophet has said:

مَنْ زَارَ قَبْرِیْ وَجَبَتْ لَهُ شَفَاعَتِیْ

'Whoever (of my followers) visits my tomb it is binding on me to plead for (Mercy and Forgiveness) on his (or her) behalf (on the Day of Judgment).'

We should love our Prophet and pay greater respect to him than to any other human being including our parents.

CHAPTER 2
PRAYER الصلوة

The second principle of Islam is to offer the Obligatory prayers five times a day. Prayer is the act of worshipping Allah according to the teachings of the Holy Prophet. The essential requisites for offering prayer are:

1. The worshipper must be a Muslim.
2. The worshipper's clothes and body must be free from all impurities.
3. The place where the prayer is to be offered should be pure and clean.
4. The part of the body between the navel and the knees of a male worshipper must be fully covered, and the whole body excepting the hands and face of a female worshipper.
5. The worshipper must face the Ka'ba in the great Mosque at Makkah and the direction of Ka'aba outside Makkah.
6. The worshipper must form the Niyyat (intention) in his or her mind of the particular prayer, Fard (Obligatory) or Sunnat or Nafil (Optional), he or she is about to offer.
7. The worshipper must observe the times and rules prescribed for the respective prayers. The worshipper must have performed the Wudu (ablution).

8. The worshipper must have performed Ghusl (the washing of the whole body), if he or she was in a state of grave impurity.

Note: In order to keep the body clean from dirt and all minor impurities and to be ever ready for prayer, a Muslim must wash the private parts of his or her body with water whenever any impure matter issues from the body.

Before one can perform the prayer we must perform the Wudu or Ghusl as we shall see in the next chapter.

CHAPTER 3

WUDU الوضئ

Wudu is the act of washing those parts of the body which are generally exposed.

We perform the Wudu in the following manner:

STEP 1

First, make sure that the water with which you are going to perform Wudu is pure, clean and fresh (not used before) and its color taste and smell are unchanged.

Then form and have the full intention of performing the Wudu for offering prayer:

Recite: 'Bismillaahir-Rahmaamr-Raheem', i.e. in the Name of Allah, the Beneficent, the Merciful.

STEP 2

Then wash your hands up to the wrists three times, passing the fingers in between each other.

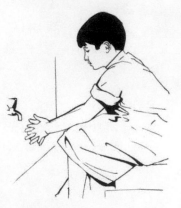

STEP 3

Then cleanse your mouth with brush or finger and gargle with water three times.

STEP 4

Then rinse the nostrils thrice with water.

STEP 5

Wash the face from the forehead to the chin bone and from ear to ear three times.

STEP 6

Then wash the right arm followed by the left up to the elbows three times.

STEP 7

Then wipe over the whole head with wet hands.

STEP 8

Pass the wet tips of the index finger inside and the wet tips of the thumb outside the ears, and pass over the other surface of the hands over the nape and the sides of the neck.

STEP 9

Then wash the feet up to the ankles, the right foot first and then the left, taking care to wash in between the toes, each three times.

The Obligatory Acts in the performance of Wudu

The obligatory acts are four:

1. Washing the face.
2. Washing both the arms up to the elbows.
3. Brushing over a quarter of the head with wet hands.
4. Washing both feet up to the ankles.

Note, if the water to be used for Wudu is stagnant, one should make sure that the cistern measures ten cubits by ten cubits and is full of water.

If a person wears impermeable footgear after the performance of the Wudu it is not necessary to remove it for a fresh Wudu. One may just pass over it wet fingers as if one were tracing lines on it. Travelers can take advantage of this concession for three days and three nights, others for one day and one night.

CHAPTER 4

GHUSL غسل

Ghusl becomes obligatory after:
1. Sexual intercourse
2. Discharge or effusion of semen
3. Completion of menses and confinement.

The obligatory conditions that must be fulfilled for a valid performance of an obligatory Ghusl are:
1. To rinse the mouth thoroughly so that all the parts are cleaned properly.
2. To rinse the nose right up to the nasal bone.
3. To wash all the parts of the body thoroughly, including the hair.

The best way of performing an obligatory Ghusl is:
1. Make an intention (niyyat) to cleanse the body from grave impurity at the time of performing the bath.
2. Wash both hands up to the wrists thrice.
3. Then the private parts must be washed thoroughly thrice.
4. Remove any filth from any of the parts of the body.
5. One should then perform an ablution (as above).
6. One should lastly wash thrice all the parts including the hair thoroughly.

Chapter 5

TAYAMMUM تیمم

When a person is sick or access cannot be had to water, one may perform what is called Tayammum in place of Wudu or Ghusl.

The essential steps to perform the Tayammum are:

STEP 1

To have the intention in mind to perform the Tayammum for the removal of impurities.

STEP 2

To strike pure earth lightly with the palms of both the hands.

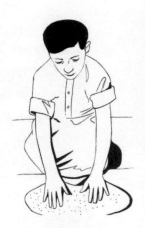

STEP 3

To pass the palms of the hands over the face once.

STEP 4

To strike again lightly pure earth with the palms of both the hands.

STEP 5

Rub alternately from the tips of the fingers to the elbows, the forearms and the hands.

CHAPTER 6
MISCELLANEOUS NOTES

The acts or circumstances which make the Wudu void are:

1. Answering the call of nature, discharge of semen or issue worm or sandy stone or any impure matter from the front or the hind private parts.
2. The passage of wind from the hind private part.
3. The act of vomiting a mouthful of matter.
4. Emission of blood, pus or yellow matter from a wound, boil, pimple, etc., to such an extent that it passes the limits of the mouth of the wound, etc.
5. Loss of consciousness through sleep, drowsiness, etc.
6. Temporary insanity, fainting fit, hysteria or intoxication.
7. Audible laughter during prayer.

The same occurrences nullify Tayammum also, but in addition Tayammum is nullified as soon as the cause for performing it is removed, i.e. if the sick person recovers, or, if recourse has been taken to it for lack of water, and access to water becomes possible.

The following three acts are forbidden without the performance of Wudu or Tayammum as the case may be:

1. Prayer.
2. Walking round the Holy Ka'ba in Makkah.

3. Carrying or touching the Holy Qur'an.

Note: Children who have not attained the age of puberty i.e. about seven years, can carry the Holy Qur'an for the purpose of studying.

Besides the cleansing the body, Wudu conveys an inner meaning of spiritual cleanliness and purity, i.e. freedom from sins is the main object of religion. It is preferable, therefore, to recite the following prayer after the Wudu:-

اَ للّٰهُمَّ اجْعَلْنِىْ مِنَ التَّوَّ ابِيْنَ وَ اجْعَلْنِىْ مِنَ الْمُتَطَهِّرِيْنَ

Allaahummaj'alnee minattawwaabeen waj'alnee minal mutatahhireen.

'O, Allah! Make me from among those who repent for their sins and from among those who keep themselves pure.'

CHAPTER 7

AZAN اذان

Azan is the first call to prayer and is uttered in a loud voice to announce to the faithful that it is time for the Obligatory prayer and to invite them to offer the same. The Azan is recited in a loud voice by the Muezzin (the crier) facing the direction of the Ka'ba in the following words which are said in the order mentioned:

1. Allaahu Akbar ﺍَﷲُ ﺍَﻛْﺒَﺮُ

    Allaah is Most Great (four times).

2. Ash-hadu al laa ilaaha illallaah. ﺍَﺷْﻬَﺪُ ﺍَﻥْ ﻵَ ﺍِﻟٰﻪَ ﺍِﻻَّ ﺍﷲ

    I bear witness that there is none worthy of being worshipped except Allah. (Twice)

3. Ash-hadu anna Muhammad-ar-rasoolullah

    ﺍَﺷْﻬَﺪُ ﺍَﻥَّ ﻣُﺤَﻤَّﺪَ ﺭَّﺳُﻮْﻝُ ﺍﷲِ

    l bear witness that Muhammad is the Apostle of Allah' (Twice)

4. Hayya 'alas-Salaah ﺣَﻰَّ ﻋَﻠَﻰ ﺍﻟﺼَّﻠٰﻮﺓِ

    Come to prayer (turning the face alone to the right and saying it twice).

5. Hayya Alal-falaah   حَىَّ عَلَى الْفَلَاحِ

Come to Success (turning the face alone to the left and saying it twice).

6. Allaahu Akbar   اَللهُ اَكْبَرُ

Allah is Most Great (twice).

7. Laa ilaaha illallaah   لَآاِلَهَ اِلَّا اللهُ

There is no Deity but Allah (once).

Fajr Azan

The following phrase is added after line 5 in the Azan of the early morning prayer:

As-salaatu khairum minannaum   اَلصَّلوةُ خَيْرٌ مِّنَ النَّوْمِ

Prayer is better than sleep (to be said twice).

CHAPTER 8

IQAMA اقامت

Iqaamat is the second call to prayer and is uttered immediately before the beginning of the Obligatory prayer (fard). It is similar to Azan but with the addition of the sentence after line 5 of the Azan.

'Qad qaamatis-Salaah' قَدْ قَامَتِ الصَّلٰوةُ

Prayer has indeed begun', to be uttered twice.

CHAPTER 9

THE OBLIGATORY AND ESSENTIAL FACTORS OF PRAYER

The Obligatory Factors in a prayer are seven in number:
1. To say Takbeer-e-Tahreemah.
2. Qiyam, i.e. standing erect and placing the right hand upon the left, below the navel.
3. To recite some verses from the Holy Qur'an.
4. Rukoo', i.e. bowing down in such a way as to grasp the knees with the hands keeping the back in a straight line so as to form a right angle with the legs.
5. Sajdah, i.e. prostrating in such a way that both the palms of the hands, the forehead, the nasal bone, the knees and the toes of both feet touch the ground; there must be sufficient space between the arms and the chest and the legs and the belly so that they do not touch each other but remain separate.
6. Qa'dah, i.e. sitting down in a reverential posture, keeping the right foot erect on the toes and the left one in a reclining position under the rumps.
7. To signify the completion of prayer by word or action.

The observance of the following six points is very essential (Waajib) in any prayer.

1. To say takbir-e-tahrima; 'Allaahu Akbar'.

2. To recite the opening chapter of the Holy Qur'an (the Fatiha).

3. To recite any of the other chapters or at least three consecutive verses of the Holy Qur'an.

4. The recitation of the opening chapter must precede the recitation of any other chapter or three consecutive verses of the Holy Qur'an.

5. To avoid a pause between the recitation of the opening chapter and any other chapter or three consecutive verses of the Holy Qur'an.

6. To assume all the postures correctly, i.e. undignified haste must not be practiced in changing the postures and reasonable pauses must be observed at each stage.

PERFORMING THE PRAYER
A complete description of the prayer

A prayer consists of two, three or four Rak'ats, and a Rak'at is performed thus:

<u>**STEP 1**</u>

Stand erect, facing the direction of Ka'bah in Makkah. The feet must be 4-6 inches apart. People with physical disabilities are exempt from holding positions they cannot manage comfortably.

After having made the Niyyat, i.e. the intention in your mind of whatever prayer you are about to offer and preferably uttering it aloud to yourself, raise both hands up to the ears and, say, 'Allaahu Akbar.'

The eyes of the worshipper should rest on the place where you will make sajda.

Bring them down and place the right hand upon the left below the navel. In Qiyaam (standing position) hands are folded underneath the navel, the right palm resting on the left palm with fingers stretched in normal straight position.

Then recite:

سُبْحَانَكَ اللّٰهُمَّ وَ بِحَمْدِ كَ وَ تَبَا رَكَ ا سْمُكَ وَتَعَالٰى جَدُّكَ وَلَآ اِلٰہَ غَيْرُكَ

Subhaanakallaa-humma wa bihamdika wa tabaarakasmuka-
wa ta'aalaa jadduka wa laa ilaaha ghairuk.

'All Glory be to Thee, O Allah! and Praise be to Thee;
blessed is Thy name and exalted Thy majesty; and there is none worthy of worship besides Thee.'

اَعُوْذُ بِا للهِ مِنَ ا لشَّیْطٰنِ ا لرَّ جِیْمِ

A-oozu billaahi minash shaitaanir-rajeem.

'I betake myself to Allah for refuge from the accursed Satan.

بِسْمِ اللهِ الرَّ حْمٰنِ ا لرَّ حِیْمِ

Bismillaahir Rahmaanir-Raheem.

'(I begin) in the name of Allah, the Beneficent, the Merciful.

Then recite the Opening Chapter of the Holy Qur'an (the Fatiha);

اَلْحَمْدُ لِلّٰهِ رَبِّ الْعٰلَمِیْنَ (۱) الرَّحْمٰنِ الرَّحِیْمِ (۲) مٰلِكِ یَوْمِ الدِّیْنِ (۳)اِیَّاكَ نَعْبُدُ وَاِیَّاكَ نَسْتَعِیْنُ (۴) اِهْدِنَا الصِّرَاطَ الْمُسْتَقِیْمَ(۵)صِرَاطَ الَّذِیْنَ اَنْعَمْتَ عَلَیْهِمْ (۶) غَیْرِ الْمَغْضُوْبِ عَلَیْهِمْ وَلَا الضَّآلِّیْنَ (۷)آ مِیْنْ

Alhamdu lillaahi Rabbil-'aalameen ar-Rahmaanir-Raheem, Maaliki Yaum-id-Deen, Iyyakana-budu wa iyyaka nasta'een; ihdinassiraatalmustaqeema siraatalla-zeena an'amta 'alaihim ghairil maghdoobi 'alaihim wa-lad-daalleen. Aameen!

'All Praise is due to Allah, Lord of the worlds. The Beneficent, the Merciful, Owner of the Day of Judgment. Thee alone we worship and Thee alone we ask for help. Show us the straight path, the path of those who Thou hast favoured, not (the path of) those who earn Thine anger nor (of) those who go astray. Amen!'

Immediately follow this up by reciting some passage from the Holy Qur'an, which should not consist of less than three consecutive verses. For this purpose any one of the small chapters may be selected, as for instance, the chapter termed 'The Unity' :

قُلْ هُوَاللّٰهُ اَحَدٌ ۱ ۞ اَللّٰهُ الصَّمَدُ ۲ لَمْ يَلِدْ وَّلَمْ يُوْلَدْ ۳

وَلَمْ يَكُنْ لَّهُ كُفُوًا اَحَدٌ ۴

Qul huwallaahu Ah ad, Allaahus-Samad, lam yalid wa lam yoolad, wa lam yakul lahoo kufuwan ahad.

'Say: He is Allah, the One, Allah, the eternally Besought of all! He begets not, nor is He begotten. And there is none comparable unto Him.'

Note: If a small chapter be recited, it is preferable to precede it by: 'Bismillaahir-Rahmaanir-Raheem.'

STEP 3

Then, saying 'Allaahu Akbar,' bow down in Rukoo' and say thrice:

سُبْحَانَ رَبِّىَ الْعَظِيْم

Subhaana Rabbiyyal-Azeem

'How Glorious is my Lord, the Great!

In Ruku (bowing position), the eyes of the worshipper are pinned to his toes. He is to bend himself in such a way that the legs and the thighs are in straight line flexed backward and the trunk and the head should be at right angle to the legs. He should not lean on the knees.

STEP 4

Again assume the standing position, letting the hands remain on the sides and say:

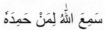

سَمِعَ اللهُ لِمَنْ حَمِدَه

Sami'Allaahu liman hamidah.

'Allah has listened to him who has praised Him;

رَبَّنَا لَكَ ا لْحَمْدُ

Rabbanaa lakal-hamd.

Our Lord! Praise be to Thee.

STEP 5

Then, saying 'Allaahu Akbar', prostrate and perform the Sajdah, saying thrice:-

سُبْحَانَ رَبِّىَ الْاَ عْلى

Subhaana Rabiyyal-A'laa.

'All glory be to my Lord, the Most High.'

In Sajdah (prostration), the worshipper should first touch his nose on the floor and then the forehead. The thumbs of the worshipper are almost in a straight line with the eyes and the fingers should be together and are almost below the ears. The elbows must not touch the floor.

The feet should never leave the floor. In the Sajdah (prostration), the worshipper's feet should rest on the fingers and toes. At no time should the feet leave the ground. The fingers and toes are so curved that the inner sides are firmly positioned on the floor.

STEP 6

Then raise yourself and, sitting for a while in a reverential posture, termed Jalsah, say once:

اَللّٰهُمَّ اغْفِرْ لِىْ وَارْحَمْنِىْ

Allaahummaghfirlee warhamnni

'O Allah! forgive me and have mercy upon me.'

In Jalsah (sitting position), the eyes should look at the lap and the hands rest on the thighs, the fingers not falling on the knees. It is important that one must sit in upright position fully before resuming the second Sajdah.

43

STEP 7

Then perform the second Sajdah exactly in the same way as the first one.

STEP 8

This finishes one Rak'at. Then say 'Allaahu Akbar', and, standing erect once again, repeat all that you had done in the performance of the first Rak'at *without* reciting 'Subhaanakallaa-humma' and 'A-oozu billaahi' which are meant to be recited in the first Rak'at only.

STEP 9

After completing the second Sajdah of the second Rak'at sit back up saying Allaahu Akbar,' and remain sitting in the reverential posture called Qa'da-tul-Oolaa (first sitting) or Qa'da-tul-Aakhirah (last sitting) as the case may be.

In Qa'dah (sitting position), the back should be in a straight line with the head. The body should rest firmly on the left foot and the right foot should be propped on the fingers and toes with the inner side touching the floor.

Then recite the tashahhud:

اَلتَّحْيَاتُ لِلّٰهِ وَالصَّلَوٰةُ وَالطَّيِّبَاتُ اَلسَّلَامُ عَلَيْكَ اَيُّهَاالنَّبِىُّ وَرَحْمَةُاللهِ وَبَرَكَاتُهٗ ۖ اَلسَّلَامُ عَلَيْنَا وَعَلٰى عِبَادِاللهِ الصَّالِحِيْنَ ۖ اَشْهَدُ اَنْ لَآ اِلٰهَ اِلَّااللهُ وَاَشْهَدُ اَنَّ مُحَمَّدًا عَبْدُهٗ وَرَسُوْلُهٗ ۖ

At-tahiyyaatu lillaahi wassalaa-waatu wattaiyyibaatu assalaamu 'alaika ayyu-hannabiyyu wa rahmatullaahi wa barakaatuhu assalaamu 'alainaa wa 'alaa ibaadillaahis-saaliheen, ash-hadu al laa ilaaha illallaahuwa ash-hadu anna Muhammadan abduhoo wa rasooluh.

'All reference, all worship, all sanctity are due to Allah. Peace be on you, O Prophet, and the Mercy of Allah and His blessings. Peace be on us and all the righteous servants of Allah. I bear witness to the fact that none is deserving of worship except Allah and I bear witness to the fact that Muhammad is His Servant and Apostle.'

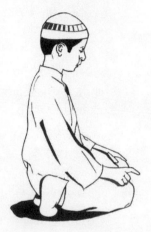

In Qa'dah (sitting position), while reciting (with the movement of the lips without raising the voice) the Tashahhud (ash-hadu al laa ilaaha...), the three fingers after the index finger of the right hand should be folded slightly into the palm of the hand and the index finger should be pointing straight upward as in the illustration and at reaching ILLALLAAH in the tashahhud the right hand should come back to its original position like the left one.

STEP 10

If more than two rak'ats are to be performed eg three rak'ats in Maghrib or four rak'ats in Zohar, then after completing the tashahhud you must stand up again whilst saying, 'Allahu Akbar.' and complete one or two rak'ats, as the case may be, starting from step 8.

STEP 11

After completing the second Sajdah of the final rak'at, sit down in the reverential posture called Qa'datul-Akhira, which is also obviously adopted if the prayer consists of two Rak'ats only. In the reverential posture, recite the tashahhud as in step 9 and then continue by reading the salawat:

اَللّٰهُمَّ صَلِّ عَلَى سَيِّدِ نَا مُحَمَّدٍ وَّ عَلَى اٰلِ سَيِّدِنَا مُحَمَّدٍ كَمَا صَلَّيْتَ

عَلَى سَيِّدِنَاۤ اِبْرَا هِيْمَ وَ عَلَى اٰلِ سَيِّدِنَاۤ اِبْرَ اهِيْمَ اِنَّكَ حَمَيْدٌ مَّجِيْدٌ اَللّٰهُمَّ

بَارِكْ عَلَى سَيِّدِنَاۤ مُحَمَّدٍ وَّ عَلَى سَيِّدِنَاۤ مُحَمَّدٍ كَمَا بَا رَكْتَ عَلَى سَيِّدِ نَاۤ

اِبْرَاهِيْمَ وَعَلَى اٰلِ سَيِّدِ نَاۤ اِ بْرَا هِيْمَ اِنَّكَ حَمَيْدٌ مَّجِيْدٌ

Allaahumma salli alaa sayyidinaa Muhammadinw waalaa aali sayyidinaa
Muhammadin kamaa sallaita alaa sayyidinaa Ibraahima wa alaa aali
sayyidinna Ibraahima innaka Hameedum Majeed. Allaahumma baarik
alaa sayyidinaa Muhammadinw wa alaa aali sayyidinaa Muhammadin
Kamaa baarakta alaa sayyidinaa Ibraahima wa alaa aali sayyidinaa
Ibraahima innaka Hameedum Majeed.

'O, Allah! Bless our leader Muhammad and his descendants
as Thou blessed our leader Abrahim and his descendants: verily.
Thou are the Praiseworthy, the Glourious.'

Then recite the following du'aa:

اَللّٰهُمَّ اِنِّى ظَلَمْتُ نَفْسِىْ ظُلْمًا كَثِيْرًا وَّلَا يَغْفِرُ الذُّنُوْ بَ اِلَّا اَنْتَ

فَاغْفِرْلِىْ مَغْفِرَ ةً مِّنْ عِنْدِ كَ وَارْحَمْنِىْ اِنَّكَ اَنْتَ الْغَفُوْرُ الرَّحِيْمُ ۞

Allaahumma innee zalamtu nafsee zulman kaseeranw, wa Laa
yaghfiruz-zunooba illaa anta faghfirlee maghfiratam min indika
warhamnee, innaka antal Ghafoorur-Raheem.

'O Allah! I have been extremely unjust to myself and none
grants forgiveness against sins but Thou; therefore forgive me
Thou with the forgiveness that comes from Thee and have mercy
upon me. Verily, Thou art the Forgiver, the Merciful.'

46

STEP 12

Then turn your face to the right and say the Salaam:

اَلسَّلَامُ عَلَيْكُمْ وَرَحْمَةُ اللهِ

Assalaamu 'alaikum wa rahmatullaah,

'Peace be upon you and the mercy of Allah.'

While turning the face towards the right side, the eyes of the worshipper should be fixed upon his right shoulder.

STEP 13

Then turn your face to the left and repeat the same.

While turning the face towards the left side, the eyes of the worshipper should be fixed upon his left shoulder.

Here the prayer is completed.

Sajdatus-Sahw

If a worshipper omits any of the essentials of a prayer or suspects that he or she has performed more than the required number of Rukoo's, Sajdahs, Rak'ats, etc., then he or she should perform one Salaam after reciting Tashahhud and, making two Sajdahs, should again recite Tashahhud, Salawaat and Du'aa and complete the prayer with the usual two Salaams. (This is called Sajdatus-Sahw).

The acts that nullify one's prayer are:
1. Talking.
2. Doing any three acts in succession.
3. Emission of impure matter from the body or the annulment of Wudu in any way.
4. Drinking or eating during prayer.
5. Turning the chest away from the direction of Ka'ba.
6. Committing breach of any of the obligatory factors of a prayer.
7. If the body between the navel and the knees becomes uncovered in the case of males, or any part of the body excepting the hands and the face in the case of females.

Classification of Prayer

There are six kinds of prayer
1. Fardul-'ain, i.e. the compulsory prayer that must not be missed any account whatsoever. This obligatory prayer must be offered at any cost for if one fails to do so he or she will be liable to severe punishment. The nature of its importance is evident from the fact that if one denies its obligatory nature, he or she is classed as an unbeliever.

2. Fardul-kifaayah is the kind of prayer which should preferably be offered by all those present at the time, but one at least out of the group must offer it to free the others from responsibility; for example, if any one individual from amongst the inhabitants of locality where the death of a Muslim has taken place or from those who join the funeral procession to the cemetery offers the 'Funeral prayer', the obligation of all concerned is fulfilled.

3. Waajib is a prayer which comes next in rank to Fardul-'ain in accordance with the importance attached to it by the Holy Prophet.

4. Sunnat-ul-mu'akkadah is the class of prayer which the Holy Prophet used to offer daily without fail and has ordered his followers to do so. One is liable to be questioned for neglecting to offer the same without some very cogent reasons.

5. Sunnatu'ghairil-mu'akkadah is the kind of prayer which the Prophet offered occasionally and desired his followers to do so.

6. Nafl is a voluntary prayer and it is commended for the uplift of one's soul, and for the acquirement of spiritual benefits.

Fard Prayers

There are only two kinds of Fard prayers:
1. The daily obligatory prayers.
2. The special congregational prayers on Fridays.

The daily Obligatory prayers are five in number:
1. Salaatul-Fajr, i.e. the early morning prayer which must be offered after dawn and before sunrise.
2. Salaatuz-Zuhr, i.e. the early afternoon prayer, the time for which commences immediately after the sun begins to decline and lasts till it is about midway on its course to setting.
3. Salaatul-'Asr, i.e. the late afternoon prayer which must be offered sometime after the sun is about midway on its course to setting until a little before it actually begins to set.
4. Salaatul-Maghrib, i.e, the evening prayer which must be offered between the sunset and the disappearance of the light similar to the light at dawn, which follows when the red glow from the horizon in the West has vanished.
5. Salaatul-'Ishaa, i.e. the night prayer which must be offered any time after the time for Salaatul-Maghrib comes to an end, and before the break of dawn, but it should preferably be offered before midnight.

The number of compulsory Rak'ats in the five daily Obligatory prayers are:
1. Two in Salaatul-Fajr (the early morning prayer).

2. Four in Salaatuz-Zuhr (the afternoon prayer).
3. Four in Salaatul-'Asr (the late afternoon prayer).
4. Three in Salaatul-Maghrib (the evening prayer).
5. Four in Salaatul-'Isha (the night prayer).

Sunnatul-mu'akkadah should be offered along with each of the five daily Obligatory prayers. The number of Rak'ats is as follows:
1. Two before the Fard of Saalatul-Fajr.
2. Four before and two after the Fard of Salaatuz-Zuhr.
3. None before or after the Fard of Saalatul-Asr.
4. Two after the Fard of Salaatul-Maghrib.
5. Two after the Fard of Salaatul-'Ishaa.

Sunnatu-ghairil-mu'akkadah can also be offered in the daily prayers. They are:
1. Four Rak'ats before the Fard of Salaatul 'Asr.
2. Four Rak'ats before the Fard of Salaatul Ishaa.

Waajib-Ul-Witr

Waajib-ul-Witr prayer should be offered after the Fard and Sunnatul-mu'akkadah of Salaatul-'lshaa. It consists of three Rak'ats. It differs from other prayers in this respect, that, in the third Rak'at, before one bows down for the performance of Rukoo', one should say: 'Allaahu Akbar', raising the hands up to the ears, and after placing them in the former position below the navel, one should recite the following du'aa called Du'aa'-ul-Qunoot:

اَللّٰهُمَّ اِنَّا نَسْتَعِيْنُكَ وَ نَسْتَغْفِرُ كَ وَ نُوْمِنُ بِكَ وَ نَتَوَكَّلُ عَلَيْكَ وَنُثْنِىْ عَلَيْكَ الْخَيْرَ وَنَشْكُرُ كَ وَلَا نَكْفُرُ كَ وَ نَخْلَعُ وَ نَتْرُ كَ مَنْ يَّفْجُرُكَ اَللّٰهُمَّ اِيَّاكَ نَعْبُدُ وَلَكَ نُصَلِّىْ وَ نَسْجُدُ وَ اِلَيْكَ نَسْعٰى وَ نَحْفِدُ وَنَرْجُوْا رَحْمَتَكَ وَنَخْشٰى عَذَا بَكَ اِنَّ عَذَا بَكَ بِا لْكُفَّا رِ مُلْحِقٌ ۝

Allaahumma innaa nasta'eenuka wa nastaghfiruka wa nu'minu bika wa natawakkalu 'alaika wa nusni alaikal khaira wa nashkuruka wa laa nakfuruka wa nakhla'u wa natruku manyyafjuruk; allaahumma iyyaaka na'budu wa laka nusallee wa nasjudu wa ilaika nas'aa wa nahfidu wa narjoo rahmataka, wa nakhshaa azaabaka inna azaabaka bilkuffaari mulhiq.

'O Allah! We beseech Thy help and ask Thy pardon and believe In Thee and trust In Thee, and we praise Thee In the best manner and we thank Thee and we are not ungrateful to Thee, and we cast off and forsake one who disobeys Thee. O Allah! Thee alone do we serve and to Thee do we pray and make obeisance and to Thee do we flee and we are quick (in doing so), and we hope for Thy mercy and fear Thy chastisement; surely Thy chastisement overtakes the unbelievers'.

Salaatul-Janaazah

Salaatul-Janaazah is offered with the congregation in the following.

STEP 1

The body of the deceased is placed in a coffin with its face turned towards the Ka'ba and the imam standing by its side with the intention (Niyyat) of offering Salaat-ul-Janaazah for that particular dead person raises both hands up to the ears and says 'Allaahu Akbar', the congregation following his lead. The usual Niyyat for the Salaatul-Janaazah is:

نَوْيْتُ اَنْ اُوَدِّىَ لِلَّهِ تَعَالَى اَرْبَعَ تَكْبِيْرَ اتِ صَلٰوةُ الْجَنَا زَةِ الثَّنَآ ءُلِلَّهِ تَعَالَى وَالصَّلٰوةُ لِلرَّسُوْلِ وَالدُّعَآ ءُ لِهٰذَا لُمَيِّتِ (اَوْلِهٰذِهِ الْمَيِّتِ) اِقْتَدَيْتُ بِهٰذَا لْاِ مَا مِ مُتَوَ جِّهًا اِلَى جِهْةِ الْكَعْبَةِ الشَّرِ يْفَةِ

Navaitu an uwaddiya lillaahi ta'aalaa arba a takbeeraati saalatiljanaazati, ath-thanaau lillaahi ta'aalaa was- salaatulirrasooli wad-du-'aau lihaazaal mayyiti (lihaazihil mayyiti. in case the deceased is a female) iqtadaitu bihaazal-lmaami mutawajjihan ilaa jihatil Ka'ba-tish-Shareefah.

'l intend to offer for Allah, the Sublime, four Takbeers of Funeral Prayer, Praise for Allah, the Sublime, and Blessings (of Allah) for the Apostle and prayer for this deceased person; l adopt the lead of this lmam, with my face turned in the direction of the honoured Ka'bah.'

STEP 2

The Imam and the congregation then join their hands below the navel and recite:-

سُبْحَانَكَ ا للّٰهُمَّ وَ بِحَمْدِكَ وَتَبَارَكَ اسْمُكَ وَتَعَالَى جُدُّكَ وَجَلَّ ثَنَاُئكَ وَلَآ اِلٰهَ غَيْرُكَ

54

Subhaana Kallaahumma wa bihamdika wa tabaarakas- muka wa ta'aalaa jadduka wa jalla thanaa'uka wa laa ilaaha ghairuk.

STEP 3

The Imam and the congregation then say 'Allaahu Akbar' (this time without raising their hands). and recite the salawat as given in (L) Item of 3rd part of question (L) in the section on "Performance of prayer'.

The Imam and the congregation then say 'Allaahu Akbar', as in (3) and if the deceased had attained the age of puberty, then the following "Du'aa":-

اَ للّٰهُمَّ ا غُفِرْ لِحَيِّنَا وَ مَيِّتَنَا وَ شَاهِدِنَا وَغَا ئِبِنَا وَ صَغِيْرِنَا وَ كَبِيْرِنَا

وَذَكَرِنَا وَأُنْثَانَا اَ للّٰهُمَّ مَنْ اَ حْيَتَهُ مِنَّا فَاَ حْيِهِ عَلَى

الْا سْلَا مِ وَمَنْ تَوَفَّيْتَهُ مِنَّا فَتَوَ فَّهُ عَلَى ا لْا يْمَانِ

Allaahummaghfir li hayyinaa wa mayyatinaa wa shaahidinaa wa ghaa'ibinaa wa saqheerinaa wa kabeerinaa wa zakarinaa wa unthanaa; Allaahumma man ahyaitahu minnaa fa ahyihee alalislaam waman tawaffai-tahoo minnaa fatawaffahu 'alal lmaan.

Meaning; 'O Allah! Pardon our living and our dead, the present and the absent, the young and the old, the males and the females. O Allah! he (or she) to whom Thou accordest life, cause him to live in the observation of Islam, and he (or she) to whom Thou givest death, cause him to die in the state of Iman.

If the deceased is a minor and a boy, then the following Du'a:-

اَ للّٰهُمَّ اجْعَلْهُ لَنَا فَرْ طًا وَّ ا جْعَلْهُ لَنَا اَ جْرَ ا وَّ ذُخْرَا وَّ جْعَلْهُ لَنَا

شَافِعًا وَّمُشَفَّعًا

Allaahummaj'alhu lanaa faratanw waj'alhulanaa ajranw wa zukhranw waj'alhu lanaa shaafi'anw wa mushaffa'aa.

Meaning; 'O Allah! make him our forerunner, and make him, for us, a reward and a treasure, and make him, for us, a pleader, and accept his pleading. If the deceased is a minor and a girl, then the following Du'a:

$$اَللّٰهُمَّ اجْعَلْهَا لَنَا فَرْطًا وَّ ا جْعَلْهَا لَنَا اَ جْرًا وَّ ذُخْرًا وَّ جْعَلْهَا لَنَآ$$
$$شَافِعَةً وَّمُشَفَّعَةً ط$$

Allaahummaj'alhaa lanaa faratanw waj'alhaa lanaa ajranw wa
zukhranw waj'alhaa lanaa shaa-fi'atanw wa mushafia'ah.

'O Allah! Make her our forerunner, and make her, for us, a reward and a treasure, and make her, for us, a pleader and accept her pleading.'

Then the imam and the congregation say 'Allaahu Akbar', as in step 3. Then turning their faces alone to the right they say, 'Assalaamu 'alaikum wa rahmatullaah'. Then they turn their faces alone to the left and say: 'Assalaamu 'alaikum wa rahmatullaah'.

Salaat-Ul-Musaafir

This is the traveler's prayer. When one is traveling with the intention of going forty eight miles or more away from home, one should offer two Rak'ats of Fard prayers for those which comprise four, and continue to do the same after one's arrival at a destination if one does not intend to prolong his or her stay there for fifteen days or more. One should continue to read the Sunnah and Nafl prayers as normal

When reading in congregation behind an Imam then you should not shorten your prayer to two Rakats but follow the Imam as normal. There is no shortening of the Maghrib prayer.

Salaatul-Jumu'a

Salaat-ul-Jumu'ah is the Friday congregational prayer and cannot be offered alone. Consequently, an Imam (Leader) is necessary to lead the prayers. The Imam first of all delivers a Khutbah in two parts consisting of praise to Allah and prayers of blessing for the Holy Prophet and some admonition to the congregation. He then prays to Allah for the welfare of all Muslims. After that he leads two Rak'ats of the Fard of Jumu'ah and all other follow him, as usual in congregational prayers.

When choosing the most suitable person to lead the prayer, the one most conversant with Islamic theology among those present should be requested to lead the prayers.

The method of offering the Congregational prayer is as follows:

The Imam stands in front of the congregation facing the direction of the Ka'bah, and all the other worshippers stand in lines behind him and follow his lead, i.e. they stand when he stands, perform Ruku when he does it, and so on.

A person offering his prayers with a congregation should recite everything excepting the Opening Chapter of the Holy Qur'an followed by some other passage from it which the Imam recites on behalf of the congregation.

Notes:

Only the Fard of each prayer is offered in a congregation, and not Sunnat or Nafl. If one misses congregation for any prayer, one should offer it alone or, if possible, join or arrange to have another congregation; but if one misses the congregation of Salaatul-Jumu'ah one should offer by oneself the usual Fard Salaatuz-Zuhr.

Salaatut-Taraaweeh

Salaatut Taraweeh consists of twenty Rak'ats and is offered in ten Salaams of two Rak'ats each, each night in the month of Ramadan only after the Obligatory 'Isha prayers. It is very commendable to complete the whole Qur'an by reciting consecutive portions of it in each of its Rak'ats after the recitation of the Suratul-Fatiha, and thus finish the whole Qur'an by the end of the month of Ramadan.

Waajibul 'Id

Eidul-Fitr and 'Eid-ul-Adha prayers consist of two Rak'ats. They are offered in the congregation thus:

1. The Imam as usual stands in front of the congregation, and facing the direction of the Ka'bah and having the intention of offering the particular prayers says, aloud; 'Allaahu Akbar', and the congregation follows his lead.

2. Then the Imam and the congregation place their hands below the navel as usual, and recite 'Subhaanakallaahumma' (to the end) inaudibly, then, at short intervals, Perform three 'takbeers',i.e. say 'Allaah-u-Akber', thrice, raising the hands up to the ears and letting them remain at the sides at the end of each "takbeer". After the end of third 'takbeer' the hands are placed below the navel then Imam recites Suratul-Fatiha (the Opening Chapter) and some other chapter or passage from the Holy Quran audibly and finishes the Rak'at in the prescribed manner.

3. In the second Rak'at, the order is reversed, for the recitation of Qur'anic passages are made first and then the Imam and the congregation perform the three 'takbeers' as in the first one, and then saying 'Allaahu Akbar' for the fourth time, bow down in the Ruku' and complete the prayer as usual.

4. After the prayer is over, the Imam mounts the pulpit and delivers two Khutbas or sermons. At the time of "Eidul-Fitr" the imam explains the commandments regarding the payment or distribution of 'Sadaqaatul-Fitr' and on

the occasion of "Eidul-Adha" the commandments about
the sacrifice of animals.

Nafl Prayers

There are various special optional (Nafl) prayers. These are:

1. Salaatul-lshraaq, which consists of two or four Rak'ats and may be offered after sunrise.

2. Salaatud-Duhaa, which consists of two to eight Rak'ats and may be offered any time after the   Salatul-lshraaq till the Sun's declination.

3. Salaatu-Tahiyya-til-Masjid, which consists of two Rak'ats and may be offered on entering a mosque.

4. Salaatut-Tahaij'ud, which consists of four to twelve Rak'ats and may be offered after midnight preferably after having slept for some time. This prayer has been specially recommended in the Holy Qur'an for attaining spiritual progress.

5. Salaatul-Kusoofain, which consists of two Rak'ats and may be offered during the eclipse of the sun or the moon.

Forbidden Times for Prayer

One is forbidden to offer either Fard, Sunnat or Nafl prayers at the following times:
1. The time when the Sun is rising.

2. The time when the Sun is at its zenith.

3. The time when the Sun is setting.

There are other times when one should not offer the Nafl prayers such as:
1. The interval between the offering of the Fard of Salaatul-Fajr and the rising of the sun.

2. After the Iqaamat is called for any congregational prayer in a mosque.

3. The time between the offering of the Fard of Salaatul-'Asr and the setting of the sun.

4. The time between the setting of the sun and the offering of the Fard of Maghrib prayers.

5. The time between the Imam's getting up from his place for delivering the Khutbah, i.e. the sermon and the completion of Friday congregational prayers.

6. At the time of any Khutbah, e.g. Friday. 'id, etc.

7. The time between the Fajr prayer and the 'id prayers.

8. After the 'id prayers at the premises where the same have been offered.

9. At the time of Hajj in 'Arafat after the Zuhr and 'Asr prayers are offered together.

10. The time between the Maghrib and 'Ishaa prayers at Muzdalifa.

11. When there is very little time left for offering the Fards of any of the daily prayers.

12. When one feels the need to answer a call of nature.

Miscellaneous

The recitation of Suratul-Fatiha and some other chapter or passage of the Holy Qur'an is made audibly in:
1. The two Rak'ats of the Fard of Salaatul-Fajr.
2. The First two Rak'ats of the Fard of Salaatul-Maghrib.
3. The First two Rak'ats of the Fard of Salaatui-'lshaa.
4. The two Rak'ats of Salaatul-Jumu'ah.
5. The two Rak'ats of both 'Id prayers.
6. In all the twenty Rak'ats of the optional Taraaveeh prayers in the month of Ramadan.
7. In the three Rak'ats of the Waajibul-Witr prayers in the month of Ramadan only.

Recitation of the Holy Qur'an is made inaudible in all the Rak'ats of the Fard of Salaatuz-Zuhr and Salaat-ul-'Asr and the last one and two Rak'ats respectively of the Salaatul-Maghrib and the Salaatul-'lsha. The Fatiha alone is recited in these Rak'ats as also in the last two Rak'ats of Salaatuz-Zuhr and Salaat-ul-'Asr.

The prayers that should be offered in congregation are:
1. All Fards of the five Obligatory prayers.
2. The Fard of Salaatul-Jumu'ah.
3. Both the 'id prayers.
4. Salaatut-Taraaveeh in the month of Ramadan.
5. Waajib-ul-Witr in the month of Ramadan only.
6. Funeral prayer.
7. Salaatul-Kusoof.

CHAPTER - III

Zakat

Zakat is charity or Islamic Alms-Fee. Zakat is the amount in kind or money which a Muslim of means must distribute among the deserving every year. Zakat is obligatory on all Muslims who have in their possession for one complete year gold of the minimum weight of seven and a half tolas or silver of the minimum weight of fifty-two and a half tolas (a tola is equivalent in weight to 11.6363 gm.). The annual rate of Zakat on gold or silver is 2.5%.

Zakat is obligatory not only on gold or silver but also on camels, cattle, goats and all articles of trade. Zakat is exempted on pearls and precious stones when used as ornaments for personal use but are liable to Zakat as articles of trade. On articles of trade Zakat should be calculated on the net balance of the value of the articles of trade at the end of the year.

Zakat is to be distributed among the following classes of Muslims for relieving respective wants:

1. The poor Muslims, to relieve distress.

2. The needy Muslims, to supply to implements for earning their livelihood, and those whose hearts are inclined to embrace Islam, i.e. the converts to Islam, the new Muslims to enable them to settle down and meet their emergency needs.

3. The Muslims in debt, to free them from their liabilities incurred under pressing necessities.

4. The Muslim wayfarers, if any one of them be found to be stranded in a land foreign or strange to him and stands in need of help.

5. Muslim prisoners of war, for liberating them by payment of ransom money.

6. Muslim employees appointed by a Muslim Amir for the collection of Zakat, for the payment of their wages.

7. Those engaged in the way of Allah, to defray the expenses for the defense and propagation of Islam.

8. For the obligation of Zakat to be imposed the condition is that the Zakat must be distributed among the classes of Muslims for the purposes enumerated above with the Niyyat of fulfilling the obligation of Zakat and to see to it that the recipient is made the absolute owner in his or sole right of what is given to him or her.

The moral that this institution of Zakat conveys to us is that one must not be selfish and get too fond of worldly possessions, but must always be ready and willing to help your brethren by all means at your disposal.

Sadaqatul-Fitr

Sadaqatul-Fitr is a charity, the annual distribution of which is essential (Waajib) for every Muslim who possesses on the last day of the month of Ramadan or the day of 'Eid-ul-Fitr any goods of the value which makes them liable for Zakat. A Muslim has to pay the Sadaqatul-Fitr for himself or herself and for his or her minor children.

One hundred and seventy-five and a half tolas of wheat or its equivalent value per head is the minimum amount of Sadaqatul-Fitr that a Muslim is enjoined to pay. Sadaqatul-Fitr should be given to those who merit and deserve Zakat.

It should preferably that Sadaqatul-Fitr be distributed before offering the 'Eidul-Fitr prayers, otherwise at any other time.

Those who are not entitled to receive Zakat or Sadaqatul-Fitr are:
1. Those on whom payment of Zakat is obligatory.
2. The descendants of the Holy Prophet, however poor they may be.

Note: The descendants of the Holy Prophet may accept or be given presents or simple charity but not Zakat or Sadaqat-ul-Fitr.

CHAPTER – IV

Fasting

The observation of fasts in the month of Ramadan means the act of abstaining from eating, drinking, smoking, allowing anything whatsoever to enter into what is understood to be the interior of the body, as also voluntary vomiting, self-pollution, sexual intercourse, etc. from the break of dawn till sunset.

The observation of fasts is obligatory on all Muslims excepting the infants, the insane, and the invalid. Men and women too old and feeble to bear the hardships of a fast are also exempted, but they should feed a poor and needy Muslim twice a day, or pay the amount of one Sadaqatul-Fitr for every day.

One can defer the observation of fasts under the following circumstances:

1. One is so sick that the observation of fast is likely to increase his or her sickness.

2. A woman who is suckling a child, and there is a danger of reduction in the supply of milk if she observes fasts.

3. A traveler who has reason to fear that observing of fasts will make him or her unable to prosecute the journey.

Note: As soon as one is relieved of the respective disabilities, one must observe the fasts immediately.

A woman should postpone the observation of fasts during the period of menses and when she is pregnant.

The observation of fasts is obligatory in the month of Ramadan because it is the blessed month of the year during which Holy Quran was revealed.

It may be asked if one can spread out the period of fasting and complete the observation of fasts for the required number of days 29 or 30, as the case may be at any time during the year? This is not the case as the Holy Quran enjoins upon Muslims to observe the fasts consecutively for 29 or 30 days, as the case may be, during the month of Ramadan alone. Besides, the main purpose for which the observations of fasts has been made obligatory will not be served if the period were spread 'out, for the training that one receives for bearing with thirst and hunger, and incidentally realising the distress of the starving poor and sympathising with and helping them would not be acquired.

The real significance of fasting consisting in the habit of self-control that it fosters and develops and thus enables one to save oneself from being an easy victim to temptation, and consequently minimizing the chances of committing sins, this in its turn will make the practice of virtue easier and lead one nearer to the Kingdom of Allah.

If one does not fast on any day during the month of Ramadan without a good reason, one will be committing a sin, but all the same he or she must fast on some other day to make amends for the omission.

The main obligatory factors for the proper observation of fasts are:
1. Conception or utterance of Niyyat, i.e. intention to fast.
2. Abstinence from all things that would nullify the fast from the break of dawn to sunset.

The usual form of Niyyat for fasting during the month of Ramadan is:

نَوَيْتُ صَوْمَ غَدٍ عَنْ اَدَآ اِفَرْضِ رَمْضَانَ هٰذِهِ السَّنَةِ لِلّٰهِ تَعَالَى

Nawaitu sauma ghadin an adaa'i fardi Ramadaana haazihis-sanati-
lillaahi ta'aa|aa.

'I intend to fast for this day in order to perform my duty towards
Allah in the month of Ramadan of the present year.'

The Niyyat (i.e. the intention) should be conceived or given
utterance to for each day preferably before the break of dawn. If
not, at any time before midday, if in the meanwhile one has
maintained the state of fasting from the time of dawn.

The main optional elements for the observation of fasts are:
1. Partaking of meals before the break of dawn.
2. Eating of three dates and drinking of water after sunset
   for signifying the end of the fast.
3. And reciting, prior to breaking the fast, the du'a.

اَللّٰهُمَّ لَكَ صُمْتُ وَ عَلٰى رِزْقِكَ اَفْطَرْتُ

Allaahumma laka sumtu wa'alaa rizqika aftartu.

'O Allah, for Thy sake have l fasted, and (now) break the fast with
the food that comes from Thee'.

The penalty for doing anything that makes a fast void without
any cogent reason is to observe sixty consecutive fasts or feed
sixty persons, besides observing the fast in place of one which he
or she has deliberately made void.

If anyone by mistake does something that makes a fast void
under a state of forgetfulness, the fast is not nullified, provided
one stop doing it the moment one remembers he or she is
fasting.

71

CHAPTER - V

AL - HAJJ

The Hajj is the pilgrimage to Makkah. The performance of Hajj is incumbent on all Muslims, at least once in a lifetime, if circumstances permit, i.e. if they are in a position both physically and materially to undertake the journey to Makkah, and make materially to undertake the journey to Makkah, and make sufficient provision for their dependents during the period of their absence.

Hajj can be defined as the pilgrimage to Makkah in the state of Ihram to be adopted at the Miqat strictly carrying out all that it imposes, observing wuqoof at 'Arafat, performing the Tawaf at Ka'bah, etc. in accordance with the prescribed laws.

Here are some key terms to note about the performance of hajj.

UMRA
Umra is the visit to Makkah at any time of the year in the state of Ihram to be adopted at Miqat, performing the Tawaf round Ka'ba in Makkah and accomplishing sa'ee in accordance with the prescribed laws.

IHRAM
By Ihram we mean the removal of sewn clothes from the body and wrapping it up in a couple of seamless sheets at the Miqat with the intention of performing 'Hajj' or 'Umra', and abstaining from all things that are unlawful for those intending to perform Hajj or 'Umra.

TAWAF
The performance of seven circuits round the Ka'bah (in Makkah) commencing from the Black Stone and having the Ka'bah on one's left is called 'Tawaf'.

SA'EE
Sa'ee signifies the act of marching to and from between the two hills of Safa and Marwa (near the Ka'bah) in accordance with the prescribed laws.

WUQOOF
Wuqoof is the stay at 'Arafat', at least for a few minutes, during the time between the declining of the sun from the meridian on the 9th of Zilhijja (the 12th lunar month) and before the dawn on the 10th of Zilhijja.

HARAM
The City of Makkah, in which the Ka'ba is situated along with a certain defined outlying territory on all its sides, is called 'Haram'.

MIQAT
The boundary lines which the pilgrims or those who want to perform 'Umra should not cross without adopting the Ihram are called 'Miqats'.

There are five Miqats in all:
1. Zul-Hulaifa or Bi'r-e-Ali, which indicates the border line of Haram for those coming from the direction of Medina.
2. Zatul-Iraq serves as Miqat for those coming from the side of Iraq or Mesopotamia.
3. Jahfa or Rabigh is the Miqat for those from Syria.
4. Quarn for those from the side of Najd.
5. Yalamlam for those from the direction of Yemen, Pakistan, India, etc.

When a male pilgrim is about to cross a Miqat, he should perform Ghusl, divest himself of sewn clothes, and wrap up the lower portion of his body in a seamless sheet and cover up the upper part with another one, keeping the head and face bare. The footgear must be such as to keep the central bones of the outer parts of his feet open. He must then offer two Rak'ats of Nafl, and lastly, he must form in his mind the Niyyat and give utterance to his intention as to the purpose of his adopting the Ihram.

The form of Niyyat for the Hajj is:

اَللّٰهُمَّ اِنِّىْ اُرِيْدَ الْحَجَّ فَيَسِّرْ هُ لِىْ وَ تَقَبَّلْهُ لِىْ وَ تَقَبَّلْهُ مِنِّى نَوَيْتُ الْحَجَّ وَاَحْرَمْتُ بِهِ مُخْلِصًا لِلّٰهِ تَعَالٰى ط

Allaahumrna innee ureedulhajja fayassirhu lee wa taqabbalhu minnee, nawaitul-hajja wa ahramtu bihee mukhlisal liilaahi Ta'aalaa.

'O Allah! I intend to perform, the Hajj. Make, Thou, the same easy for me and accept it from me. I have conceived the Niyyat for Hajj, and have adopted Ihram sincerely for Allah, the Sublime.'

If one wants to perform only 'Umra he or she should say:

اَللّٰهُمَّ اِنِّىْ اُرِيْدُ الْعُمْرَةُ فَيَسِّرْ هَا لِىْ وَ تَقَبَّلْهَا مِنِّى نَوَيْتُ الْعُمْرَةُ وَاَحْرَمْتُ بِهَا مُخْلِصًا لِلّٰهِ تَعَالٰى ط

Allaahumma innee ureedul 'Umrata fayassirhaa lee wa taqabbalhaa minnee, nawaitul 'Umrata wa ahramtu bihaa mukhiisal liilaahi Ta'aalaa

'O Allah! I intend to perform 'Umra. Make, Thou, the same easy for me and accept if from me. I have conceived the 'intention' for 'Umra and have adopted the Ihram for it, sincerely for the sake of Allah, the Sublime.

The intention or Niyyat for performing Hajj and 'Umra together is:

اَللّٰهُمَّ اِنِّىٓ أُرِيْدَ الْحَجَّ وَ الْعُمْرَةَ فَيَسِّرْبُهُمَا لِىْ وَ تَقَبَّلُهُمَا مِنِّى نَوَيْتُ الْحَجَّ وَ الْعُمْرَةَ وَاَحْرَمْتَ بِهِمَا مُخْلِصًا لِلّٰهِ تَعَالٰى

Allaahumma ureedulhajja wal 'Umrata fayassirhumaa lee wa taqabbalhumaa minnee nawaitul Hajja wal 'Umrata wa ahramtu bihimaa mukhlisal liilaahi ta'aalaa.

'O Allah! l intend to perform both Hajj and 'Umra. Make, Thou, the same easy for me and accept them from me. I have conceived the intention for both Hajj and 'Umra and have adopted the ihram to perform both Hajj and 'Umra only for the sake of Allah, the Sublime.

After one has given utterance to one of the Niyyats, one should say aloud (these words should be perfectly committed to memory as one will have to recite them again and again, sitting, standing, mounting and dismounting.

لَبَّيْكَ اَ للّٰهُمَّ لَبَّيْكَ لَبَّيْكَ لَا شَرِيْكَ لَكَ لَبَّيْكَ اِنَّ الْحَمْدَ وَالنِّعْمَةَ لَكَ وَالْمُلْكَ لَا شَرِيْكَ لَكَ

Labbaik Allaahumma labbaik; Labbaik: laa shareeka laka labbaik, innal–hamda wan ni'mata laka wal mulka laa shareeka lak.

'Here I am at Thy service, O Allah! Here l am at Thy service. Here I am at Thy service; There is no partner unto Thee; Here I am at Thy service. Verily, to Thee the glory, the riches and the sovereignty of the world. There is no partner to Thee.

The things that become unlawful for those adopting the Ihram and remain as such till the object for which the Ihram has been adopted is accomplished are:

1. Hunting or aiding and abetting it.
2. Sexual intercourse or its preliminaries.
3. Cropping or shaving of hair or paring of nails.
4. Covering of head or face in any way whatsoever.
5. Use of gloves or socks.

6. Wearing of any kinds of sewn clothes or underwear.
7. Using any perfume or perfumed preparation.
8. Deliberate smelling of perfume or applying it to any part of the body or the sheets covering it, or even keeping it in on one's person. (If any aroma of perfumes applied before the conception of Niyyat remains, it does not matter, for it is permissible).
9. Killing or even dislodging and throwing away lice if they happen to find their way on one's person or the sheets covering it.

The points of difference between the adoption of Ihram by men and women are:
1. That a woman can wear sewn clothes.
2. She can cover her head (as matter of fact she should cover her head in the presence of all men excepting her husband, as also whilst offering prayers).
3. She should not put on a veil in such a manner that the fabric may touch her face.
4. She can put on socks or gloves.
5. All the other things which are unlawful for a man are also unlawful for her.

Note: A women should not utter 'labbaik' etc. aloud but should say the same in a subdued voice.

TAWAF

The points to be observed in the performance of Tawaf are:

1. The performer of Tawaf should stand towards that corner of the Ka'bah where the Black Stone is embedded in its wall in such a manner as to have it on one's right and then give utterance to the Niyyat of performing it in the words:

$$اَللّٰهُمَّ اِنِّى اُرِيْدُ طَوَافَ بَيْتِكَ الْمُحَرَّمَ فَيَسِّرْ هُ لِىْ وَ تَقَبَّلْهُ مِنِّىْ$$

Allaahumma innee ureedu tawaafa baitikalmuharrami fayassirhu lee wa taqabbalhu minnee

'O Allah! I intend to perform the Tawaf of Thy consecrated premises. Make. Thou, the same easy for me and accept it from me.

2. Then facing the Black Stone and raising the hands with palm outwards, one should say:

$$بِسْمِ اللهِ وَ الْحَمْدُ لِلّٰهِ وَ اللهُ اَكْبَرُ وَالصَّلٰوةُ وَالسَّلَامُ عَلٰى رَسُوْلِ اللهِ$$

walhamdu lillaahi wallaahu Akbar wassalaatu wassalaamu 'alaa Rassoolillaah.

'I begin in the name of Allah, and all Praise is due to Allah and Allah is Most Great, and peace and blessings be on Allah's Apostle.'

3. If possible one should approach the Black Stone and give it a kiss, but if it be not feasible, then one should give it a flying kiss, and recite the Du'a:-

77

اَللّٰهُمَّ ا غْفِرْ لِیْ ذُنُوْ بِیْ وَطَهِّرْ لِیْ قَلْبِیْ وَ ا شْرَ حْ لِیْ صَدْرِیْ وَ
يَسِّرْلِیْ اَمْرِیْ وَعَافِنِیْ فِيْمَنْ عَا فَيْتَ

Allaahummaghfirlee zunoobee wa tahhir lee qalbee Washrah lee
sadree yassir lee amree wa aafinee fee man 'aafait

'O Allah; forgive me my sins and purify my heart and expand
my chest (give me spiritual illumination) and make my task
easy and preserve me among those Thou hast preserved.

4. Then one should proceed towards the Gate of Ka'ba
saying:

اَللّٰهُمَّ اِيْمَانًا بِكَ وَ تَصْدِ يْقًا بِكِتَا بِكَ وَ وَفَآ ءُ بِعَهْدِ كَ وَ اِتِّبَا عًا
لِّسُنَّةِ نَبِيِّكَ مُحَمَّدٍ صَلَّى ا للّٰهُ تَعَا لٰى عَلَيْهِ وَسَلَّمَ وَ اَ شْهَدُ اَنْ لَّآ اِلٰهَ اِ
لَّا ا للّٰهُ وَ حْدَهُ لَا شَرِ يْكَ لَهُ وَ اَ شْهَدُ اَنَّ مُحَمَّدًا ا عَبْدُ هُ وَ رَسُوْ لُهُ
اٰمْنْتُ بِا للّٰهِ وَ كَفَرْتُ بِا لُجِبْتِ وَ ا لطَّا غُوْ تِ

Allaahumma imaanam bika wa tasdeeqam bikitaabika wa wafaa'am
bi 'ahdika wa Ittibaa'an li sunnati nabiyyika Muhammadin,
sallallaahu ta'aalaa 'alaihi wasallama, wa ashhadu al laa ilaaha ill-
Allaahu wahdahoo laa shareeka lahoo wa ashhadu anna
Muhammadan 'abduhoo wa Rasooluhoo Aamantu billaahi wa kafartu
bil-jibti wattaaghoot.

'O Allah! (l am performing this) with complete faith in thee
and Belief in the truth of Thy Book and in the fulfillment of
my pledge to Thee, and in the wake of the Sunnat of Thy
Prophet Muhammad, may peace and blessing of Allah be
upon him'. l bear witness to the fact that there is no God but
Allah, Who has no partner, and that Muhammad is His
bondman and Prophet. I have faith in Allah and do not
believe in evil spirits and ghosts.

Note: The act of kissing the Black Stone and reciting the du'a
is called 'Istilam'.

5. Then, having the Ka'bah on one's left, one should take a complete round of it, remembering Allah all the while or reciting du'aa (a and b of 3) in the same way as before. This completes one circuit.

Note: One may kiss, if possible the south-west corner of Ka'bah which is called Rukne Yamani.

6. One should perform seven rounds in the manner described.

7. After the completion of seven rounds one should stand near the gate of Ka'bah and pray for Allah's blessings.

8. Lastly, one should offer two Rak'ats of Sunnatut-Tawaf, preferably near Maqam-e-Ibrahim, a spot just near the Ka'bah.

The culpable acts during the performance of Tawaf are:
1. Being without ablution.

2. Uncovering of more than a quarter part of any limb of the body which must be kept covered.

3. Performing the Tawaf either by supporting oneself on someone's shoulder or mounted, without any cogent reason.

4. Performing the Tawaf in a sitting posture, without any cogent reason.

5. Performing the Tawaf with the Ka'ba on one's right.

6. Performing the Tawaf round the Ka'bah exclusive of Hatim (Hatim is the name for the portion of land in the North of Ka'bah which was left out when the Ka'bah was rebuilt).

7. Performing a lesser number of circuits than seven.

Acts that are not permissible during the performance of Tawaf are:

1. Discussion of mundane matters.The performance of Tawaf in an impure garb.

2. The disregard of Ramal which signifies marching briskly, moving the shoulders with chest out, like the gait of a soldier, in the first three circuits of the Tawaf of 'Umra.

3. The disregard of Iztiba'a which denotes the act of removing the sheet from the right shoulder and passing it under the right armpit to place on the left shoulder, thus keeping bare the right arm in the Tawaf of 'Umra.

4. Omission of Istilam.

5. Pauses between the circuits of Tawaf (Of course if the Wudu is made void or a congregation of an Obligatory prayer is ready, one may discontinue the circuits to perform the Wudu or to join the congregation and complete them later on).

6. The failure to offer two Rak'ats of Nafl after the completion of each Tawaf, i.e. seven circuits of the Ka'bah (if the time be, however, one when it is not permissible to offer the prayers, one is allowed to defer the same till the completion of the second Tawaf)

SA'EE

These are the steps to perform Sa'ee.

SAFA

In order to perform the Sa'ee one should make your way to Safa and after arriving there recite:

اَبْدَاءُبِمَا بَدَ ءَ اللّٰهُ بِهٖ اِنَّ ا لصَّفَآ وَالْمَرْ وَةَ مِنْ شَعَآ ئِرِ اللّٰهِ فَمَنْ حَجَّ الْبَيْتَ اَوِاعْتَمَرَ فَلَا جُنَا حَ عَلَيْهِ اَ نْ يَّطَّوَّفَ بِهِمَا وَ مَنْ تَطَوَّعَ خَيْرًا فَاِ نَّ اللّٰهَ شَا كِرٌ عَلَيْمٌ ط

Abda'u bima bada' Allahu bihi, innas-Safa wal Marwata min sha'a-
'irillihi, faman hajj-al-baita awi'tamara fala J'unaha 'alaihi anyyat-
tawwafa bihima wa man tatawwa'a khairan fa innallaah Shakirun
'Aleem.

'I commence with that with which Allah commenced. Surely Safa and Marwa are prominent symbols of Allah. Hence there is no blame on one who performs the Hajj of the House (of God) or 'Umra it he (or she) marches to and from between them (Safa and Marwa), and one who does good of one's own accord, verily Allah is Responsive, Aware.'

Then, raising the hands to the shoulders, one must say:

Allahu Akbar (thrice), and La ilaha illallahu wallahu Akbar wa lillahilhamd.

INTENTION

Then one should give utterance to his or her Niyyat in the words:

اَ للّٰهُمَّ اِنِّى اُرِ يْدُ ا لسَّعْىَ بَيْنَ ا لصَّفَآ وَ الْمَرْ وَةِ فَيَسِّرْ هُ لِىْ وَ تَقَبَّلْهُ مِنِّىْ ط

Allahumma inni ureedus-Sa'ya bainas-Safa wal Marwati fayassirhu lee
wa taqabbalhu minnee.

'O Allah! I intend to perform the Sa'e between Safa and Marwa. Make, Thou, the same easy for me and accept it from me.'

MARCHING BETWEEN GREEN SPOTS

Then one should march towards Marwa, reciting du'as all the way. When one reaches a green spot one should march quickly till one reaches another green spot, and in between those spots one should recite the following Du'a:

رَبِّ اغْفِرْ وَ ارْحَمْ وَ تَجَاوَزْ عَنْ مَا تَعْلَمُ وَتَعْلَمُ مَالَا نَعْلَمُ إِنَّكَ اَنْتَ الْأَعَزُّ الْأَكْرَمُ ۥ اَ لّٰلهُمَّ ا جْعَلْهُ حَجًّا مَّبْرُوْرًا وَسَعْيًا مَشْكُوْرًا وَذَنْبًا مَغْفُوْرًا ۥ

Rabbighfir warham wa tajaawaz 'ammaa ta'lamu wata'lamu maalaa na'lam innakaantal A'azzul-Akram; Allaahummaj-alhoo hajjammab-rooranw, wa sa yammashkooranw wa zam bammaghfoora.

'O Allah! forgive me and have mercy upon me and pass off (my sins) of which Thou are Aware, and Thou knowest that of which we have no knowledge; verily Thou art the Most Honourable, the Most Exalted. O Allah! make it (for me) a Hajj that is acceptable (to Thee) and an effort that is granted and (a means of) forgiveness of sin!

MARWA

Arriving at Marwa one should face Ka'bah and pray for blessings (this completes one turn).

Then one must go back to Safa in the same manner, marching quickly between the two green spots, reciting du'as, etc., and when Safa is reached one must again face the Ka'bah and pray for blessing (this will complete the second turn).

One must take seven such turns, and at the accomplishment of the seventh, when one arrives at Marwa and offers up the prayer one is said to have accomplished the Sa'ee.

The Performance of Hajj

In order to performe the Hajj one must complete the following steps:

1.   As soon as a pilgrim approaches the boundary line of the Holy Land, i.e. the Miqat, he or she enters the state of Ihram with all its accompaniments.

2.   On reaching Makkah the pilgrim goes to the the Ka'ba in the Grand Mosque and then performs an optional tawaf, called Tawaf-ul-Qadoom.

3.   On the 8th day of Zilhijja the pilgrim goes to Mina, before the time of Salatuz-Zuhr, a town three miles from Makkah, and spends there the rest of the day and the whole night of the 9th Zilhijja.

4.   After the early morning prayer of the 9th Zilhijja, the pilgrim proceeds to 'Arafat, a place about seven miles from Makkah, and stops anywhere in the Mauqafs (staying places) in the area surrounding the Jabal-e-Rahmat, (i.e., the Hill of Mercy) in the remembrance of Allah.

5.   Just after the sunset of the 9th Zilhijja the pilgrim leaves the Mauqaf without offering Salatul-Maghrib, and proceeds to Muzdalifa, a place between Mina and 'Arafat, where he or she offers Maghrib and Isha prayers.

6.   The pilgrim then proceeds from Muzdalifa after the early morning prayers of the 10th of Zilhijja (collecting at least 49 pebbles from there) and comes to Mina.

7.   The pilgrim then takes up seven pebbles, and holding each between the index finger and the thumb of the right hand, throws them one by one at the pillar called Jamratul-'Uqubah on the same day, i.e., the 10th Zilhijja.

8. The pilgrim then, if he or she can afford, makes a sacrifice of a goat or a sheep or joins six others in the sacrifice of a camel or a bull, and shaves off preferably the whole head or at least a quarter head, or crop the hair equally all over the head, if the pilgrim be male, and in the case of a female pilgrim, she should cut off at least an inch of her hair.

9. The pilgrim then leaves off the state of Ihram and proceeds to Makkah on the same day and performs the Tawaf, called Tawaf-ul-lfada, after which the pilgrim offers two Rak'ats of Sunnat prayers.

10. The pilgrim then accomplishes the Sa'ee.

11. The pilgrim, then returns to Mina and spends there the night of the 11th of Zilhijja.

12. After the midday of the 11th and the 12th of Zilhijja the pilgrim approaches in the order mentioned, the pillars called Jamra-tul-Oola, Jamratul-Wusta and Jamratul-'Uqubah, and throws seven pebbles against each of them, reciting at each throw: 'Bismillahi Allahu Akbar.' If a pilgrim stays on the 13th of Zilhijja as well, he or she throws seven pebbles at the pillars as on the two previous days.

13. The pilgrim then returns to Makkah after the Salatuz-Zuhr on the 12th of Zilhijja. Before leaving Makkah for one's own country, the pilgrim performs a departing tawaf, called Tawaf-ul-Wida.

Notes:

1. During one's stay at Makkah one may perform, as many tawafs as one can, for the performance of tawafs is the best form of worship during that period.

2.   One can also perform 'Umra as many times as one likes by going out of Makkah to Tan'eem (a place about three miles from Makkah) and adopting the Ihram there, return to Makkah and perform the tawaf and sa'ee as is usual for 'Umra.

UMRA

In order to perform the 'Umra one should in the first instance:

1.   Adopt the Ihram at the Miqat in accordance with the prescribed laws.

2.   After proceeding to Makkah one should betake himself or herself to Ka'ba and affecting the Iztiba'a, one should form and give utterance to the Niyyat for Tawaf and commence the performance of the same.

3.   One should take care to perform the first three circuits in the style of Ramal. However women are exempt both from Iztiba'a and Ramal.

4.   After the completion of the three circuits, the remaining four are performed in the normal manner and one should then offer two Rak'ats of Sunna-tut-Tawaf.

5.   One should then preferably proceed to the well of Zamzam and drink a little water.

6.   From there make your way to Safa and complete the Sa'ee according to the prescribed method.

7.   The performance of 'Umra is completed after the accomplishment of the Sa'ee. Now if one wants to perform the Hajj in the very Ihram, one may maintain the same; but if one does not want to do so, one should shave off at least a quarter or preferably the whole head or crop the hair all over the head. The pilgrim is then free

from all the impositions and restrictions that the state of Ihram imposes.

Hajj and 'Umra can be performed in the same state of Ihram, in which case the pilgrim should not leave off the state of lhram after the performance of 'Umra till the completion of Hajj. When the Hajj and 'Umra is performed in the same state of Ihram, it is called Qiran.

When the 'Umra is performed in the month of Hajj and then Ihram is removed and re-donned on the 7th of Zilhijja at Makkah for the second time for Hajj, it is called Tamattu'. One who performs Qiran or Tamattu' is bound to sacrifice a goat or sheep or join six others in the sacrifice of a camel or a bull, or observe ten fasts, three before Hajj and seven after its performance.

If one performs Hajj alone and not Umra, it is called lfrad. The sacrifice of an animal is not obligatory on one performing the Hajj alone, i.e., lfrad.

If anyone of the essential observances in connection with Ihram, Tawaf or Sa'ee are transgressed, one is liable for penalties in the shape of either sacrificing a goat or a sheep, or distributing alms.

After performing the Hajj, it is very commendable for a pilgrim to pay a visit to the Mausoleum, of the Holy Prophet at Medina, and standing there in a reverential posture facing the tomb of the Great Prophet, to say:

اَلسَّلَا مُ عَلَيْكَ اَيُّهَا النَّبِىُّ وَ رَحْمَةُ اللهِ وَ بَرَ كَا تُهٗ

اَلسَّلَا مُ عَلَيْكَ يَآ نَبِىَّ ا للهِ

اَلسَّلَا مُ عَلَيْكَ يَآ حَبِيْبَ اللهِ

اَلسَّلَا مُ عَلَيْكَ يَآ خَيْرَ خَلْقِ اللهِ

اَلسَّلَا مُ عَلَيْكَ يَآ شَفِيْعَ ا لْمُذْنِبِيْنَ

اَلسَّلَا مُ عَلَيْكَ وَعَلَى اٰلِكَ وَ اَصْحَابِكَ وَ اُمَّتِكَ اَ جْمَعِيْنَ

Assalamu 'alaika ayyu- han-Nabiyyu wa rahmatullahi wa barakatuhu,
Assalamu 'alaika ya Rasoolallah! Assalamu 'alaika ya Nabi-Allah!
Assalamu 'alaika ya Habib Allah Assalamu 'alaika ya khaira-khalqillah!
Assalamu 'alaika ya Shafi'-al-muznibeen! Assa- lamu 'alaika wa 'ala
alika wa as-habika wa ummatika ajma'een

'Peace be on you, O Prophet (of Allah)! and His mercy and His blessings. Peace be on you, O Apostle of Allah! Peace be on you O Prophet of Allah! Peace be on you, O Beloved of Allah! Peace be on you, O Best in the (whole) Creation of Allah! Peace be on you, O Pleader for the sinners (before Allah)! Peace be on you and your descendants and your companions and all your followers.'

PART III

Poetry

God is only One

And has no partner or son,

He has made us and everything,

All beasts, all fowls, all birds that sing,

The sun, the moon, the starry sky,

The land, the sea, the mountains high.

He knows whatever we think or act,

By Him is seen the real fact.

And only He does what He wills,

He makes, He keeps, He saves, He skills.

Forever the same, no age, no youth,

He is Perfection, He is Truth.

Almighty, All-Seeing, Wise,

He hath not form or shape or size.

But Self-Existing is our Lord,

And is always to be adored.

God is Just

Our God is Just, and loves the right,

The wrong is hateful to His sight.

To all His creatures He is Kind,

He gave us reason that we might

Know good from bad, wrong from right.

This is the first to light our path,

To gain His grace and shun His wrath.

But gift of reason varies far,

Some wise and others foolish are.

The eyes of mind our passion dims,

And reason oft is quenched by whims.

A Second Guide

For second guide we have the men

Of larger mind and wider ken,

Who could from God a message get,

His Law before the people set.

We call them Prophets, know you well,

Coming events they could foretell.

No nation was without such guide,

To warn them and from sins to chide.

Each Prophet taught in his own sphere

To worship God and Him to fear.

But thousands of such Prophets came,

Of whom we know not the name,

Of some well-known I mention make,

The Lord God Bless us for their sake!

Job, Jacob, Joseph, Abraham,

Elias, David, Solomon,

Lot, Moses, Aaron, Ishmael,

Hud, Noah, Jesus, Daniel;

With Adam first and Muhammad last,

Between the two all others pass.

Their minds were brighter than our own,

But otherwise all flesh and bone;

God did not in them incorporate.

They were but men and separate.

Books of God

The Books of God, a third guide form,

And us of His Commands inform,

God sent them through His Prophets great

Repealing older by the late;

The Qur'an now the Law in force,

The other Books have run their course.

Judgement Day

In all these Books its plainly said,

The graves will once give up their dead;

A new life God will give to men.

Who made us once will quicken again.

That day we shall, to judgment brought,

Be called to answer what we wrought,

And shall be judged by Faith we had,

And work we did good or bad.

The good shall get a festive treat–

Everlasting bliss and heavenly seat,

Where such the pleasure, such the mirth

We've never dreamt of on this earth.

The bad shall go to hell and fire,

And suffer pains and torture dire.

But sense of guilt to conscious mind

Is more than all the pains combined

While sense of having pleased our Lord

Is greatest bliss and highest reward.

The Five Pillars

The Qur'an teaches us to pray

Our Lord God five times a day;

To fast the days of Ramadan lent,

To give aims to the indigent;

To visit Makkah once in life,

And to make for God every strife.

End here the Muslim Laws in brief,

May God guide all to this belief.

Sayyed Muhammad

The Prophet of Islam

The crown of creation set with richest gems,

Diamonds and rubies in value beyond ken,

Unequalled in brilliance, unique of kind,

Art thou, O Great Prophet to all mankind,

Truthful by nature and of most saintly mien,

All called thee the Trusty, the Al-Ameen.

Most loving to children, courteous to all,

To animals tender, alike to great and small;

Never on earth a nobler soul had trod,

Never had another showed a true to God.

O sweetest flower that ever on earth did bloom,

Matchless alike in divine beauty and perfume,

O whitest lily human eyes have seen,

O loveliest rose that in the world has been,

All nature join in homage, all men adore

Thee who brought light to a darksome world;

Thee whose teachings are as a necklace of pearls

Which when worn does radiant beauty impart,

Adding luster to body, to soul and to heart.

Ya Rasoolallah, our dearest friend and guide,

May God's eternal blessings with thee abide.

From the Arabian deserts thou sounded thy call

To the worship of God, the Lord of all,

From the Arabian deserts thou taught mankind,

How the truest knowledge of God to find.

Thy words flew as lightning the whole world around,

Of Truth and Light they did fully abound,

And nations, acknowledging the power of their sway

Did find and follow the most truthful way.

In the wake of thy words true piety did spring,

And great knowledge and virtue did truly bring.

Never on earth a better soul was born,

Never the world did a purer soul adorn.

Man was fast sinking in idolatry and sin

When thou thy great mission did first begin.

Then in place of darkness thou Light did give.

And taught mankind the noblest way to live;

And reformed the world as never before.

And unique blessings on it did bestow.

Praise be to Allah for this favour divine

In sending thee the wicked world to refine.

Search the world though we may from pole to pole

While the great ocean of time doth onward roll,

A more perfect Prophet never can we find,

Than thee who, thank God, gave Islam to mankind.

Ya Rasoolallah, my homage I make to thee,

Ya Nabiyyallah, my love I tender thee,

My life, my all, for thee I gladly give,

Thy Divine messages shall with me for ever live.

My love for thee no bounds doth know,

In my heart thy memory shall for ever glow.

May Allah shower His choicest blessings on thee,

May Allah grant thee peace for all eternity.

M. J. MAJID

Joint Secretary,

The Ceylon Muslim Missionary Society, Colombo.

وَآخِرُدَعْوَانَ اَنِ الْحَمْدُ لِلّهِ رَبِّ ا لْعٰلَمِيْنَ

wa akhruddawana anilhamdulillahi rabbil aalameen.
'And in the end our claim is that all praise be to Allah, the Lord of the Worlds.'

CPSIA information can be obtained
at www.ICGtesting.com
Printed in the USA
LVHW09s1342210918
590914LV00001B/22/P

9 780992 633530